BRITISH RAILWAY INFRASTRUCTURE

For the Modeller and Historian

Robert Hendry

Midland Publishing

British Railway Infrastructure
Robert Hendry © 2005

ISBN 1 85780 204 7

First published in 2005 by Midland Publishing,
4 Watling Drive, Hinckley, Leics. LE10 3EY, England
Tel: 01455 254490, Fax: 01455 254495
E-mail: midlandbooks@compuserve.com

Design concept and layout
© Midland Publishing and
Stephen Thompson Associates

Midland Publishing is a division of
Ian Allan Publishing Ltd.

Printed in England by Ian Allan Printing Ltd
Riverdene Business Park, Molesey Road
Hersham, Surrey, KT12 4RG

CONTENTS

Title page: Colonel Holman Fred Stephens has entered railway folklore through the collection of light railways that he ran from the early 1900s until his death in 1931. He was one of the engineers jointly responsible for the Bere Alston & Calstock Light Railway. The line ran from Bere Alston in Devon to Callington in east Cornwall, crossing the River Tamar, which was the county boundary, at Calstock. We are looking from the Devon bank of the river towards Calstock and the viaduct in June 2003. The stones, or corbels, that project from the piers of the viaduct just below the arch, were used to support the wood shuttering or framework when the viaduct was built. The line was authorised in 1900, opened on 2nd March 1908, and closed beyond Gunnislake in 1966. The Cornish section was a reconstruction of a narrow gauge mineral line that ran from Kit Hill to a wharf on the Cornish bank of the Tamar below Calstock. The line reached the quay via an inclined plane that is out of sight to the left. The quay lines ran along the riverbank, part of the old quay being visible to the right of the small boat tied up by the bank. In a search for railway infrastructure I have visited many fascinating locations from inner city stations, loco depots and goods yards, to places of tranquil beauty such as this.

Below: A class 25, D7502, shunts S1798S, a Southern PLV or Passenger Luggage Van at Melton Mowbray on 30th July 1971. Steam had been a memory for three years, and shunting at wayside stations was on the decline, so it was pleasant to see activity, but the railway infrastructure was equally fascinating. We see wagon repair sidings to the left, a gas lamp, and rail built buffer stops. The bracketed signal post, with a red stop arm is worked by Melton station signal box, whilst the yellow distant arm is controlled by Melton Junction. The multiple balance weights on the post are necessary when a distant signal is on the same post as a stop signal. The white diamond indicates a track-circuited section. Moving to the right, there is a segmental arch overline bridge, an overhung signal box built by the LMS, some single post and 'A' frame telegraph poles, a BR enamel running-in board and 'Brutes' (BR parcel trolleys). If we look in more detail, there is the base of an old water column, a brick retaining wall, round nosed and square nosed Staffordshire blue platform edging bricks, and the 'doll' or small post on the deck of the gantry shows that there was once another arm on this signal. What was this for? Melton Junction once controlled the divergence of the Leicester and Nottingham lines. They were both main lines, and the Midland Railway believed in splitting distant signals at such junctions. The arm on the left hand post referred to the Leicester line, whilst the distant on the right hand post was for Nottingham. The relative importance of different routes at a junction is indicated by the height of their respective signal arms, and this applied to splitting distants as well as to stop signals. When both lines survived at Melton, the left hand route to Leicester was more important than the Nottingham line, so its distant arm was the higher of the two. When the Nottingham line closed, the Leicester distant was transferred from the left hand post to the position formerly occupied by the Nottingham distant below the stop arm. In the real world of signal fitters, what would actually happen is that the old Leicester arm would have been taken away, and the wire that controlled it would be connected to what had been the old Nottingham line arm.

Front cover top: 86210 *City of Edinburgh*, parallels the Oxford canal, as she races south along the Trent Valley line with an Up express in November 1986. Because railway and canal engineers faced similar difficulties of finding a suitable route that kept construction costs to a minimum, it is noteworthy how often the early railway builders followed the same route that the canal engineers had created.

Front cover bottom: Swinderby level crossing, on the former Midland line from Newark to Lincoln, characterises MR infrastructure which evolved in the 1870s, and remained little altered until the wholesale adoption of power box working and lifting barriers by BR from the 1960s, but is now fast disappearing.

INTRODUCTION

Above: During the long hot summer of 1959, when British Railways and I were both 11 years old, my parents took a holiday in North Wales, and we visited Llanfairpwllgwyngyllgogery-chwyrndrobwllllantysiliogogogoch station on the Chester & Holyhead section of the former London & North Western Railway. My father took some views of the station, and wanted to capture a train passing the incredible 57-letter name board in colour. He also wanted some cine, so I was deputed to film Stanier 'Black Five' No 44827 on an Up express. He felt the shot would be steadier if I was sitting down, and wanted to keep an eye on me for safety sake, so I was included in the composition of this slide. A few minutes later, I took my first colour slide under his instruction. It was a memorable day during a memorable summer. It shows a train in a characteristic railway environment with a low stone built platform that dated back to the nineteenth century. The white edging to the platform became universal as a result of the 'black-out' conditions of World War Two. The wooden fencing with its vertical pales was a standard North Western design, and was painted cream or white in the vicinity of platforms. Away from passenger areas, it was often creosoted to preserve it. The flowerbeds with their white edging stones were common, and a good floral display was encouraged by 'Best Kept Station' competitions. A rustic trellis, made by nailing together roughly trimmed branches, is visible between the 'Black Five' and the nameboard. The footbridge connecting the platforms was a Board of Trade requirement except at the most insignificant stations, or where a station from the dawn of the railway age had not been enlarged or altered. Given the length of the name, no fewer than five posts are required to support the nameboard.

Cine film shot by my father shows me gazing at a steam engine from my pram, so I was interested in railways at an early age, and that fascination has remained ever since. As I grew up in the fifties and sixties, I devoured the fascinating books by O S Nock, Cecil J Allen and C Hamilton Ellis on the pre-grouping railway companies. I am certain that their readable and entertaining accounts of the great railway companies played a major role in creating the railway enthusiast movement we know today, and the diverse railway library we enjoy is in no small measure due to their pioneering efforts. I read of Sir Richard Moon, F W Webb, G J Churchward, and Patrick Stirling, of Brunel's amazing broad gauge, or the rivalry between the different companies. My father had been born a decade prior to the grouping, so I was able to quiz him on Lancashire & Yorkshire 'Highfly-er' Atlantics, or North Western engines in and around Liverpool. The family moved to Rugby where his father became a general practitioner. After war service in the Western Desert and Italy in the 'Desert Rats', he too became a GP. From the age of ten, my father developed a sizable O Gauge model railway, which included correct signalling, block working and timetable operation. As a small child I was allowed to shunt wagons and later to join the operating team. In due course, I wanted to build something for the railway. Locomotives were beyond my youthful abilities, but wagons or buildings were feasible. My first efforts were crude, but my parents praised their good points and encouraged me to do better next time. Rather than blanket praise, which leads to self-satisfaction, or unhelpful criticism that can be devastating, this balanced approach encouraged me, and soon I wanted to make better models. This required practical skill and experience, but knowledge of the prototype was also essential. Although we had many railway books, the details I needed seldom appeared in company histories. My father realised this, and

when he made a station building, he went out with a notebook, tape measure and camera, and produced an exquisite model of the LNWR station building at Clifton Mill, complete down to the roaring fire in the booking office and the more meagre effort in the waiting room. When I was making models, his advice was, 'Don't guess, find out'.

Partly because my father was interested in railways and not just locomotives, but also because of this approach to modelling, he photographed carriages and wagons, signal boxes and stations as well as motive power. To do so in 'black and white' was rare, but when he took up colour photography, it was even more unusual. Given that background, I regarded railway photography in this wider context as routine. My first step behind the camera was at Llanfairpwllgwyngyllgogery-chwyrndrobwllllantysiliogogogoch station. I was eleven years old, and under his instruction, I took a photo of him standing by the station sign. When we modelled something, I learned to check our photo collection to see if there was anything useful. If not, the 1955 Modernisation plan and the more draconian 1963 Beeching plan on the reshaping of British Railways had not yet bitten too deeply, so it was easy to photograph what we needed. As the years went by, it became clear that fundamental and unwelcome changes were coming to the railway industry, and much that we had taken for granted would soon vanish. My father started to record the passing railway scene which he had known from childhood, and which was now disappearing at an accelerating rate.

With the demise of steam in August 1968, many enthusiasts hung up their cameras, but my father continued to photograph a diverse but threatened railway infrastructure, and I did likewise. Little was published on railway infrastructure, and finding rare structures was a matter of luck. I recall many trips to places that were under threat of closure or re-development. We found much of interest, but many fascinating structures went unrecorded. Some stations became firm favourites for technical or aesthetic reasons. An example of this is Glasgow Central. It had been commended to me by someone who knew it shortly after its 1906 rebuilding, and receives extended coverage in this volume. Apart from the lack of data, another problem was my father's hours of duty. Unlike the modern health service, where 'out of hours' calls to a GP are met by a centralised service, where the doctor may know nothing of the case history or possible complications of the patient he treats, my father and his colleague shared the 24 hour coverage, which meant he was on duty 50 per cent of his time. This hampered photography considerably, but meant a closer contact with patients. He would have deplored the modern impersonal service. Until his retirement, photographic trips had to be arranged for his weekend off.

The first, and sadly the only colour book my father and I worked on together, was written in 1984. It was called *The Steam Age in Colour*. It had to concentrate on motive power, as editors said that only an engine book would sell in colour. Even so, we included a few views of signal boxes, coaching stock and stations. My father felt that an all colour record on rolling stock, signalling and other aspects of railways would be invaluable to the modeller. Fifteen years after that first colour book, I was able to realise that dream with *British Goods Wagons in Colour*, and companion volumes on signalling and passenger stock. In preparing this series, the question I ask myself is, 'what views have I found useful as a modeller ?' Many views that made it into this series have been ones I needed for some modelling project. On this occasion, our subject is the railway infrastructure. What do we mean by infrastructure? A definition is required before we press on. An army adage drummed into new recruits was, 'If it moves salute it, if it doesn't, paint it'. We could adapt that advice to a railway context. 'If it moves, it's rolling stock; if it doesn't, it's infrastructure'. As a broad generalisation that will do, though it is not the whole story as there are some things that move, or have important moving parts, which are part of the infrastructure, such as locomotive coal or ash hoists, turntables or cranes.

Railway infrastructure is an immense subject. At their zenith in 1914, there were 23,701 route miles of public railway in the British Isles of which just over 3,000 miles were in Ireland, the rest being in England, Scotland and Wales. These figures were for route miles and when second, third or multiple tracks and sidings are added, the figure was 55,663 miles, or enough metals to build a double track line girdling the earth. Infrastructure included thousands of stations and signal boxes. How many stations were there ? The British Transport Commission Annual Report for 1948, records the following statistics as at 1st January 1948;

BR Route Mileage open standard gauge	19,639
BR Total Track mileage standard gauge	52,254
BR Total Track mileage narrow gauge	31
Passenger Only Stations,or passenger/parcels	1,886
Passenger and Freight Stations	4,815
Freight Only Stations	1,593
TOTAL	8,294
Motive Power Depots	393
Carriage Depots (steam stock)	252
Carriage Depots (electric stock)	18
Hump Freight Marshalling Yards	94
Flat Marshalling Yards	879

Standard gauge route mileage in 1912 had been 19,873 miles; in 1948 BR still operated 19,639 route miles. The reduction in total mileage compared to 1912 reveals how little had been lost up to 1948. Although there had been a few closures before the war, such as the Basingstoke & Alton Light Railway, (the setting for the Will Hay film *Oh Mr Porter*), and the narrow gauge Lynton & Barnstaple and Leek & Manifold lines, the rail network was substantially complete in 1948, and new openings had made up for the losses. The London Midland Region, with over 2,300 stations was the largest section on BR, its nearest rival being the Western Region with 1,600 stations. Interestingly, the Scottish Region, with 1,300 stations, came third, though a disproportionate number were on remote lines in the Highlands. London Transport contributed 225 stations, whilst the Irish companies, north and south of the border, the Isle of Man, and the lines which remained independent, such as the Derwent Valley Light Railway or port railways in Liverpool, Bristol or London, and lines that had closed prior to 1948, added several hundred passenger or freight depots, bringing the total to around 9,000 stations, or roughly one for every 2.5 route miles of track. Marshalling yards increase the total to 10,000 railway-owned locations. Private sidings varied from one short siding to a vast network, and added more diversity. Coalmines were a major source of private siding traffic, and as late as 1960, over 600 collieries were rail connected. By 2004, there were less than a dozen mines in operation. A total of 12,000 to 15,000 stations, marshalling yards and separate private sidings is likely. Signal boxes had peaked at around 13,000 in 1900, but with IB signals, power working of remote points and closures, had declined slightly by 1948.

BR inherited 20,023 steam engines in 1948, divided into some 490 classes, the numbers varying from one-off examples such as the Lickey banker, to 863 of the GWR 57xx pannier tanks (including examples built under BR). Unlike locomotives, with such large classes, there were no classes of identical stations. Buildings might be to standard designs, but each station varied. This was not a whim by the civil engineer, but because the station had to suit its location. It might be on straight track, or on a curve; it could be in a cutting, on level ground, or on an embankment. It might even be on a viaduct, or underground. There could be a level crossing or a road bridge. Even if two stations were identical when new, one might attract heavy traffic and be enlarged. The other might remain quiet. Although BR had 20,000 engines, it only had 490 classes of motive power. Its 8,294 stations were in effect 8,294 classes. That statistic is daunting enough. Throw in marshalling yards and private sidings, each with their own peculiar characteristics and the diversity of railway infrastructure comes into focus. These figures do not include bridges, tunnels or other elements of the infrastructure. Even the slimmed down British Railways of the post-Beeching era had over 60,000 bridges. Engines could vary from a 16 ft long 0-4-0T, which was shorter than the wagons it shunted, to a 70 foot Pacific, the tender of which was bigger than some tank locomotives. Length varied four or five-fold, and weight from 20 tons to 160 tons, or eight-fold. Dramatic though these contrasts are, stations could vary from a railcar halt on a single-track branch, to Waterloo, or Manchester Victoria/Exchange, each with over 20 platforms. That is a 20-fold difference. Apply that to motive power, and engines would vary from 16 feet to 320 feet! Platforms might hold one or 15 coaches. Apply both multipliers to motive power, and our largest engine would be 4800 feet long, or the equivalent of 38 Union Pacific 'Big Boy' 4-8-8-4s placed end to end. These figures, though fanciful, put the matter in perspective.

I have seen signal boxes with five levers and with over 180 levers. I have known minor stations that were worked from an open-air ground frame and busy locations that were worked by numerous mechanical boxes. At Rugby, on the West Coast Main line, there were once 11 signal boxes controlling the station and its approaches. In some places boxes were miles apart. At Finsbury Park, on the GN main line out of Kings Cross, the signalmen in Nos 5 and 6 boxes could have thrown stones at one another, had they wished. I have stood within yards of the girder spans at the south end of the Forth bridge, and wondered how a span that would be a 'large' bridge in any other setting is dwarfed into insignificance by the massive cantilever spans that cross the Forth. When writing this book, I was tracing the course of the late lamented Ashover Light Railway at Ashover Butts, and spent some time looking for a river bridge. The abutments, which were about four feet high, were so close that you could step from one to the next. Engineers have built bridges in wood, iron, steel, stone, and concrete. They have built plate or lattice girders, bowstring girders, tubular bridges, suspension bridges, arches and cantilever bridges. The term infrastructure includes all of these items. It includes rails, sleepers, ballast and the very formation itself, such as cuttings or embankments. Most enthusiasts will have seen the early lithographs of the sheer sided Olive Mount cutting on the approach to

Above: As the effects of the Beeching Plan started to bite, it became clear that the idyllic days of the country station were numbered. My father felt it was important to make a colour record of a facet of railway life that was vanishing. On 2nd October 1965, he visited Lilbourne on the 50 mile LNWR cross country route from Rugby to Peterborough. The wooden building is to a prefabricated design introduced c1876. It was used extensively during the doubling of the Rugby & Market Harborough line in 1878, with a main building on one platform and a simple shelter on the other platform. At Lilbourne, and the adjacent station, Clifton Mill, the signal box butted on to the station building. An LNWR signal post has been used as a telegraph post. A 'strain wire' runs diagonally from the post to the ground on the right. In the 1930s, the LMS adopted the 'Hawkseye' name board. The first board the passenger saw as the train entered the station was placed diagonally to make it easier to read, as he looked out of the compartment window. The running in board at the far end of the right hand platform is positioned in this way. The peeling paint and weathered state of the inside of the signal box door show that Lilbourne has not received attention from the painters for many years. The standard LM Region station colours were red and cream, but Lilbourne carries LMS chocolate brown and light stone. The signal box name is LMS white lettering on a black ground rather than LMR red. Except for the bridge carrying the M1 in the distance and the cutting back of the valance to permit larger stock, the scene had hardly changed since 1878.

Below: Six years later, on 5th August 1971, we revisited the station, and I stood on the same spot to take this view. The rails have gone, as have the buildings. All that remains are the grass grown platforms and the brick built lamp hut at the far end of the left hand platform. The platform surface was formed of blue brick, edged with chequer pattern non-slip Staffordshire blue edging bricks. Some of the Staffordshire blues that were visible in the previous view have been dislodged and lie forlornly on the abandoned track bed. These two views encapsulate the sudden change that overcame Britain's railways, and remind us that a way of life that had been unchanged for generations vanished overnight. It was also a graphic reminder of my father's wisdom in recording such scenes before it was too late.

Liverpool (Lime Street) station. Elsewhere, they will have seen gently sloped cuttings, and may have wondered why there is this incredible variation. This is just one of the questions we will explore.

Highlighting this diversity reveals the impossibility of covering railway infrastructure in one volume. Selection is inevitable, and that raises the problem of omission. Over a dozen views examine bridges. This is probably the most comprehensive record of this subject in colour so far published, but dozens of others were considered. Work from such legendary engineers, contractors and architects as George & Robert Stephenson, H F Stephens, J W Livock, G T Andrews, Joseph Mitchell, James Miller, William Marriott, Donald Matheson, I K Brunel, C B Vignoles, F W Webb, Sir William Arrol, Sir Rowand Anderson, Sir Benjamin Baker and Sir John Fowler are covered, whilst a bridge designed by Sir Thomas Bouch, the creator of the ill-fated Tay Bridge, appears in the scale plans. Unlike the Tay Bridge, it stood for over 80 years. Sadly, the creations of many legendary engineers, architects and contractors, have been left out for lack of space. Had I included them, other scenes would have had to go. As with other volumes, the choice has been whether to cover a wide field in outline, or selected topics in depth. This allows better understanding of the subjects covered at the price of omissions. When I have been searching for data as a modeller, I have often found references in several books that duplicate one another, but stop short of the detail I want. On one modelling project, I could not find the detail I needed, but with official permission, I scrambled over the structure I wished to model, and used two reels of film in a few minutes. In this series I have opted for an 'in-depth' treatment, with the sad but inevitable result that some topics do not make it to the final selection. When we produced *British Railways Goods Wagons in Colour*, some questioned if a wagon book in colour would sell. Two reprints and a sequel, which was facetiously nicknamed 'Son of Wagons' until a final title was adopted, and further volumes on coaching stock and signalling, suggest the approach has worked for other modellers. Infrastructure is a neglected subject, and there is ample scope for 'Son of Infrastructure', so let us hope that the treatment in this volume appeals to you, the reader, and we can keep on with this series.

This book would not have been possible without the help and encouragement of many people. My first acknowledgment is to my father, the late Dr Robert Preston Hendry (1912-1991). He took colour pictures of railway infrastructure at a time when relatively few enthusiasts took colour pictures of engines. As a result, we have colour photos of a station in faded LMS paintwork in this volume. He encouraged me to do likewise. He enjoyed the friendship and respect of many railway officers from the 1950s to the 1990s, and was granted facilities not ordinarily open to the public. My Mother, Elaine Hendry (1906-1986) encouraged my interest in railways, and happily allowed family trips to be interrupted by visits to stations and other railway facilities. In more recent times, my wife Elena has joined me on photographic trips, and made many helpful suggestions. I have picked the brains of an old school friend, Clive Partridge, who has spent many years rising up the managerial tree within the industry. He has added a professional railwayman's perspective. I have asked another friend, Blair Ramsay, for a professional engineer's perspective. A sincere vote of thanks go to the railway officers without whose co-operation, many of the views in this book could not have been taken.

Below: In 1971, between my Law Finals at University, and the degree ceremony, I recorded the changing face of railways around Birmingham. The GWR Birmingham main line was a shadow of its former self, with Snow Hill station a rotting shell, and through services eroded with the electrification of the North Western lines from Euston to Birmingham, Liverpool and Manchester. When BR was formed, the Western Region had predictably adopted chocolate and cream as its regional colours. Although 23 years had elapsed since the formation of British Railways, Smallheath & Sparkbrook Station still displayed its GWR sign, although the GREAT of GREAT WESTERN RAILWAY had been painted brown in deference to the new owners. Sparkbrook had been dropped from the station name, and the unwanted word crudely obliterated in black paint. Other than these cosmetic changes, the station had altered little from its remodelling at the close of the Edwardian era in conjunction with the opening of Moor Street station and the North Warwickshire line from Tyseley to Stratford-upon-Avon. The twin towers are the lift house casings, and lattice gates open directly on to the pavement for luggage and parcels. Access doors to the lift mechanism open on to the roof. Other than for the 1970s era posters, modern life in the form of parking restriction signs, or the ubiquitous double arrow logo, are notable by their absence.

Right: Logos, such as the BR double arrow, the Esso roundel, the Shell symbol, or the LT bar and circle, are seen as a modern idea, but the Midland Railway was using this 'corporate logo' when Queen Victoria was not yet middle aged, by emblazoning a mythological winged dragon, or Wyvern on its rolling stock, its station buildings, its timetables, and even the buttons on its staff uniforms. I spotted this Wyvern in one of the cast iron spandrels supporting the canopy at Hellifield station in the 1970s. Although there are highly decorous and respectable Wyverns, and one such beast formerly graced the frontage of Derby Midland station, the Hellifield Wyvern is a particularly riotous specimen, with its tongue out, and its tail sticking backwards and upwards at a defiant angle. Clearly it was a beast with a mind of its own, a disdain for lesser neighbours, and every intention of doing exactly what it wanted. Given the formidable reputation of the Midland, it was an apposite choice for a very forceful railway. The Midland did not 'invent' the Wyvern, but acquired it when they took over the Leicester & Swannington Railway. They in turn acquired it from the heraldic arms of Leicester. Before that, it had appeared on the crest of the Earls of Leicester, and they had taken it over from the ancient kingdom of Mercia, of which Leicester was the main community. With a pedigree going back a thousand years, the Wyvern probably felt fully entitled to put out its tongue. It will be interesting to see which logos of today are still around in the year 3005 AD, and I commend readers at that date to consider this point!

Right: Traditional infrastructure was under threat in many different ways. In the 1970s, the Midland main line was still mechanically signalled, much of it dating from the quadrupling between 1875 and 1895. The MR Chief Engineer's report for 30th June 1895 commented, 'the widening between Bedford and London, including the tunnels at Elstree and Ampthill, is now completed, four parallel lines of way being thus opened for traffic between Glendon Junction and London, a distance of 75 miles'. The claim was premature as the final section was not finished until 28th July, but MR pride was understandable, as it was the longest section of continuous four-track line in the British Isles. Millbrook box is south of Bedford in what was the most prolific brick producing area in the British Isles. The dragline excavators for the clay used in brick manufacture and the tall brickworks chimneys on the skyline characterised this area for decades. This single arm bracket signal proclaims its Midland ancestry, and probably dates from the 1890s quadrupling. Although most pre-grouping companies used wooden signal arms, the Midland and the LNWR adopted pressed steel corrugated arms prior to 1914. Power box working would come, but when we visited Millbrook on 10th October 1971, like-for-like replacement of life expired semaphore signals was still taking place. The replacement tubular post has been erected, but the new arm has not been installed, nor the old Midland signal taken out of use.

Left: My father found the juxtaposition of old and new on the railways fascinating. He first visited Sandy station on the Great Northern main line when he was an undergraduate at Queen's College, Cambridge in the 1930s. He travelled by the LNWR Bletchley and Cambridge line, and would break his journey at different wayside stations. At Sandy, the LNWR and GNR shared a station with cross platform interchange. In February 1976, we visited Sandy and found this contrast between the pre-grouping swan necked gas lamp and a BR totem. It displays the operating chains that were used to ignite the incandescent mantle, and the framework used to support a BR totem. Various ways exist to light a gas lamp. One method is to turn on the gas, and hold a match or taper close to the mantle, but this is of a silk material, and can be damaged by contact with a taper, and an open gas lamp is difficult to ignite in inclement weather. In some automatic systems, a small pilot light burns continuously, and when the short chain is pulled, the gas reaches the mantle producing a bright light. When the other chain is pulled, the gas supply is cut off from the mantle. In an alternative method, pulling the chain opens the gas supply and generates a spark to ignite the gas. My father had childhood memories of such lighting, and was pleased to see it once again at Sandy.

Left: When Robert Stephenson was appointed Engineer to the London & Birmingham Railway, it was clear that the major engineering obstacles were in the 35 miles between Bletchley and Rugby. To keep to the easy gradients then desired, the line faced formidable cuttings at Denbigh Hall just north of Bletchley, and at Roade, and then Kilsby Tunnel itself. In July 1837, the first section of the L&B from London to Boxmoor opened, with an extension to Tring following in October. On 9th April 1838, the line was extended to a temporary terminus at Denbigh Hall, the section from Birmingham to Rugby opening on the same day. Passengers detrained at Denbigh Hall, and were conveyed by stagecoach to Rugby for the final leg of their journey. A limited service of through trains began on 24th June, but the full service did not start until 17th September 1838, when the temporary terminus closed, giving it the distinction of being one of the first railway stations in the world to be closed! At Denbigh Hall, the L&B crossed the ancient Roman Watling Street at an angle, necessitating a skew bridge. In the pioneering era of railways, bridges and other structures were highly decorative. This was to impress the public with the grandeur of the project. Graceful cast iron arches rest on dressed stone abutments, with a row of projecting stones, or dentils, just below the parapet. The west face of the bridge is largely unaltered, and retains the ornate iron balustrade that appears elsewhere on early portraits of the L&B. The abutment on the left hand side is backed by the embankment, but due to the skew, the right hand abutment is not backed by an embankment, so is reinforced by masonry buttresses.

Right: The inscription on the bridge recalls that 'PRIOR TO SEPTEMBER 1838, THE SOUTHERN PART OF THIS RAILWAY TERMINATED AT THIS BRIDGE WHENCE PASSENGERS WERE CONVEYED BY COACH TO RUGBY WHERE THEY REJOINED THE RAILWAY FOR BIRMINGHAM'. The memorial was financed by Sir Herbert Leon, Bart and Lady Leon of nearby Bletchley Park in 1920. A little known Victorian mansion for many years, Bletchley Park became the home of the top-secret Government Communications and Cypher School in World War Two. Its cryptanalysts were to decipher German communications up to Führer level, materially assisting the Allied war effort and saving countless allied lives. In 1838, Denbigh Hall gained brief fame as the northern terminus of what was cutting edge technology. Just over a century later, Bletchley Park was involved in cutting edge activity of a very different kind.

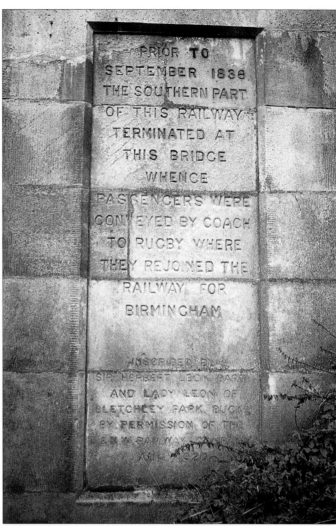

Below: By the mid-1840s, a 'Railway Mania' had developed, and the established companies threw off branch lines to 'stake out' new territory, to protect existing routes, or to handicap rivals. To enhance their prestige, they employed some of the leading architects of the day. The Doric arch at Euston was a classic example of this, but even in small towns and villages, money was lavished on stations of baronial splendour. Despite the prudent chairmanship of George Carr Glyn, a celebrated London banker, the London & Birmingham poured far more money than was necessary into building a long cross-country route from Blisworth to Peterborough. It opened as a single-track branch on 2nd June 1845, but doubling began almost at once, and was completed by September 1846. John William Livock was responsible for the main stations on the line, which were in the Tudor or Jacobean style. Oundle is a picturesque town with a celebrated public school for boys, and the station building, in dressed (or ashlar) stone with its soaring octagonal chimneys, straight edged gables, and diamond shaped roof slates, was in the Tudor theme. The projecting bay or Oriel window on the first floor was typical of Livock's work. Even in the 1950s, the population of Oundle was no more than 3,100, and the economics of creating such a magnificent building are open to question. At nearby Wansford, with a population of around 400, the case for a comparable building in Jacobean style was even more dubious. By the time Oundle station was photographed, on 15th July 1971, it had closed to regular passenger traffic, but remained open to freight and for start and end of term specials for Oundle school. Freight traffic ended in 1972.

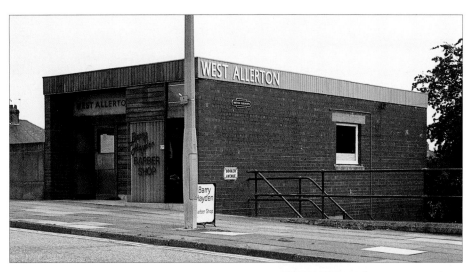

Top: We will visit Merseyside to examine the approach adopted a century later. West Allerton lies between Allerton and Mossley Hill on the line from Speke Junction and Edge Hill. When the LNWR route from Crewe to Liverpool had been opened in the nineteenth century, this area was open fields, but residential developments in the 1930s prompted the planning of a new station in 1937. A brick-built booking office fronted on to Booker Avenue, with a plate girder footbridge providing access to the four platforms. The station opened on Monday 2nd January 1939. The booking office was originally finished with dressed stone, but this was replaced by a timber and glass frontage to accommodate a barber's shop in later years.

Above: The waiting shelters were less substantial, as they were timber framed, and clad in hardboard ! The down slow waiting shelter, which bears Patent Shaft & Axletree Co makers plates, hardly differed from the day it was built when we photographed it in September 1982, which is quite a tribute to the lasting qualities of hardboard! The plans prepared by the Structures Section of the Chief Engineers Office, reveal that toilet facilities were only provided on the Down Slow platform, and then merely for gents. The down slow platform was the principal platform for commuters heading into Liverpool, and most pre-war commuters on this route would be men! On the way home, the commuters would not have a long walk to reach their own homes, so did not need a toilet, whilst women would be fewer in number, and would no doubt show greater foresight before embarking upon a journey. In modern times, such discrimination would outrage the equal opportunities lobby. By the time this view was taken, BR had eliminated any charge of discrimination. They closed the toilet.

Opposite page top: Launton station was on the LNWR-backed Buckinghamshire Railway, which ran from Bletchley to Oxford, with a branch from Verney Junction to Banbury. The Verney Junction to Islip section, on which Launton is located opened on 1st October 1850. At this date, level crossings were acceptable, and several wayside stations were located at crossings. Launton was worked by an outdoor 7-lever ground frame, which controlled the signals, whilst a gate lock lever, which was interlocked with the signals, released the gates. The locking rod runs to the crank near the pedestrian crossing, and then under the boarding to the gates. It then runs vertically from the black casing at the bottom of the gate, and via another crank, beside the fourth iron tie bar, to the end of the gate. The gateman has opened the down gates and is now opening the far gate on the Up side. The gate is a standard LNWR diagonally braced two bay gate with horizontal tie rods, and is carried on rectangular wooden gate pillars with cast iron caps. Although the Up line has been re-laid in flat bottom rail, the track through the crossing is bullhead to avoid digging up the road. The rail is secured by elastic track spikes made of silico-manganese galvanised spring steel. The spike is driven through a pre-bored hole in the sleeper until the rail is held firmly. This was the standard BR track fastening until the adoption of the Pandrol clip in 1964-65. It is better than the dog spike which was driven into the sleeper, with just a protruding lip to hold the rail, and in theory the elasticity of the curved head of the spike absorbs the pumping motion of the rail as a train passes over it, so the spike does not pull out of the sleeper. In practice, gauge retention was poor, as was resistance to rail creep, which is the tendency of rails to move in the same direction as the traffic. Six-hole BR 1 baseplates are used. At first, two elastic spikes are driven into the sleeper on the inside of the rail, and one on the outside. If rail creep occurs, or if a spike loses its grip due to a split in the timber, additional spikes can be driven in through the unused holes. A junction fishplate is required when rails of different types are joined. As the tops of the rails must be level, the bottom of the fishplate is stepped, and the holes drilled accordingly.

Opposite page bottom: The GWR shed at Westbury opened in April 1915, and closed in September 1965. It was a four road shed, with a short repair shop to the right, a turntable (out of view) and a brick built coal hole and water tank. The engines in the yard include Nos 6990 *Witherslack Hall*, 6908 *Downham Hall*, 3864 and 4697. Ash was dumped in an ash pit near the coal hole, or on the ground, and was cleared away by the rail crane and grab ahead of No 4697. The shed approach tracks are relatively free of weed. Except in the vicinity of the shed and coal hole where engineering brick is used, the ground is compacted coal dust and mud. The inclined line to the coal hole is overgrown, as is the wagon standage siding to the right of the coal hole. BR built 16 ton steel mineral wagons were commonly used for loco coal in the latter days of steam, but the use of five plank High Goods for loco coal may come as a surprise. In the section on permanent way, I referred to the two hole GWR chair which had a serrated base, and was secured to the sleepers by through bolts. The point in the foreground demonstrates GW permanent way components.

THE FORMATION

Below: Despite early ornamentation, the railway engineer had his feet planted firmly on the ground. Sweeping hills and mighty rivers were picturesque, but they were not the terrain he liked. The ideal place for a railway was dead flat, without hills or dales, without rivers, and preferably without roads, towns and cities, all of which added expense and complication. West Bank Hall, where the tracks stretch straight as an arrow across the flat Yorkshire plain would seem to be an ideal location, but without human activity, a railway serves little purpose, and whilst railways in more populated but more awkward terrain have survived, the main line of the Hull & Barnsley Railway has been a memory for more than half a lifetime. The line was built to carry coal from the South Yorkshire coalfields to Hull for export, and when Britain was the premier coal-exporting nation, millions of tons of coal flowed east to the Humber. However, the interruption of exports during World War One prompted many countries to develop their own collieries, whilst the switch from coal to oil burning shipping destroyed another important market. With its staple traffic in decline, the H&B was in financial difficulties as early as 1919. The line limped into the grouping and to BR, but the writing was on the wall. Passenger services were withdrawn between 1932 and 1955 and through freight services ended in April 1959. By January 1967 the metals lay rusting and silent, the only reason they had survived was in case they were needed to serve Drax power station which was then under development. West Bank Hall signal box, which was a short distance west of Carlton, dated from 1916, and was a replacement for an earlier structure. It was to the second H&B design with deep three pane windows. The 'X' bracing on the platform handrails was a feature of H&B boxes.

Opposite page, bottom: The River Aire meanders through this flat plain. It rises in the rugged and beautiful Pennines northwest of Skipton, and joins the northern Ouse and then the Trent, to form the imposing Humber estuary. The H&B crossed the Aire on bridge No 101, a two-span Bowstring girder with stretchers connecting the tops of the spans, the line being on a shallow embankment at this point. This structure, along with the Ouse and Hull swing bridges, three tunnels west of Little Weighton, and the discovery that some ground needed blasting rather than excavating, pushed up the cost of the line to twice the parliamentary estimate. Work was temporarily suspended due to cash shortages before the line was open, and the Hull & Barnsley was saddled with a capital debt that the traffic never warranted. Given that much of the route was through flat agricultural land, which was ideal for the railway builder, the eventual cost of £58,911 a mile made it one of the most costly lines per mile to be built, which suggests that surveying and engineering supervision was inadequate. As enthusiasts, we tend to forget that good planning prior to construction and adequate supervision when the project is under way are as crucial to success in railway building as to any other project.

Above: The flat country of the Fens that stretches from Ely to the Wash at Kings Lynn would seem ideal territory for the railway builder, but pitfalls awaited the unwary. Lying at or below sea level, the area had been subject to tidal inundation until the land reclamation schemes of the last four hundred years. A complex system of drainage canals, pumping station and barriers kept the sea at bay, and opened up a productive black peat soil to agriculture. The line from Newport (Essex) to Cambridge, Ely, Brandon and Norwich was opened jointly on 30th July 1845 by the Eastern Counties Railway and the Norfolk Railway. Both companies were part of the 1866 amalgamation to form the Great Eastern Railway. In common with other lines that touched the fens, it was not easy to build, as the reclaimed ground did not provide a firm foundation for railways or buildings. Shippea Hill, which was on the ECR section, was the first passenger station east of Ely, so was on the edge of the Fens. The GER upgraded the signalling between Ely and Wymondham in 1883, providing a series of GE/McKenzie & Holland signal boxes. Shippea Hill received an '1873 pattern' McKenzie frame. A century and a quarter of use on the soft Fenlands had left the box in parlous condition. It survived solely because substantial trussing prevented it from falling backwards into the fens. The box had warped beyond belief, as is evident from the extraordinary shape of the window frames, and maintaining the robust but sensitive locking frame in a building that lacked stability had become a nightmare. Test boring in the vicinity of the box revealed that solid rock was 60 to 80 feet below ground level in places! Sometimes modellers quip that reproducing a structure like this is easy, as there is no need to bother about verticals or horizontals, or ensure that parallel lines are truly parallel. Up to a point, this is true, but it is only some structural lines that are distorted. Others remain true. Modelling a building that has subsided, or an old timber framed coach that has bowed, in a convincing manner is in fact a considerable test of the modellers' skills, as it is all too easy to make it look like poor quality workmanship.

Below: Hilly terrain was a more common problem than subsidence, and cuttings or embankments, bridges and tunnels were needed to maintain acceptable gradients. The Great Western Railway had been conceived as the grand route between London and Bristol, but within a decade had embarked on a trunk route to the Midlands, and to the banks of the Mersey. The GWR-backed Oxford Railway was authorised in 1843, and completed the following year. The Oxford & Rugby Railway was to carry broad gauge metals on to Rugby. It reached Banbury in 1850, but by then plans had changed, and the O&R route beyond Fenny Compton was discarded in favour of the Birmingham & Oxford Junction Railway. Leamington Spa, the most important intermediate community on this new route, was located in a hollow, and the B&OJ dropped from Harbury to Leamington Spa, and then climbed for five miles from Warwick to Hatton Junction. Banking engines were allocated to Leamington shed to assist freights up Hatton Bank, part of which was in a deep cutting. Unlike the Lickey incline which had no additional tracks, a relief line was laid in to reduce congestion. The unequal separation of the relief line from the main lines is due to the

twin and single track arches of the masonry viaduct that spans the cutting. The angle at which ground is cut back is dependent on the material through which the cutting is made. Where a stable rock formation exists, cutting sides can be vertical, but where treacherous and unstable clay is found, the cutting must be at a gentle angle. With the electrification of the West Coast Main line, and reopening of the Leamington-Coventry chord for south-west to north-east services, loco hauled expresses became a rarity up Hatton bank, until 19th September 1986 when two express trains collided at Colwich Junction on the Trent Valley line. West Coast services were diverted via Coventry, and to avoid congestion between Coventry and Stechford, southwest/northeast services were diverted via Hatton and Smallheath, rejoining their correct route outside Birmingham New Street station. Bescot-based 47 535 *University of Leicester*, decked out with large arrows and numerals, growls up Hatton bank a couple of days after the accident. The second man in the cab is probably a conductor-driver as the regular driver may not have route knowledge of this section as he will not normally work over it.

Opposite page top: Stanier 'Black Five' No 45464 heads a four coach express along the GCR at the Ashlawn Road bridge near Rugby in July 1966, a few weeks before the closure of the GC as a through route. The depth and width of the cutting dwarfs the train, and reveals why the GC was so costly to build. Even more than at Hatton, the gentle slope is apparent, but there is an added reason here. When the GC was laid out, its promoters had looked back over the previous sixty years. The first trunk route to the north, the London & Birmingham had been built in 1837-38, with the Trent Valley section following a decade later. The GN main line had opened in the 1850s, and the Midland route to St Pancras in the 1860s. The LNWR quadrupled much of its route in the 1870s and 1880s, with the Midland following suit in the 1880s and 1890s. On average, traffic to the north required an additional pair of tracks every ten years. With urban development, further widening of existing routes was uneconomic, so the London Extension was planned for double track, but with the formation and stations laid out to make quadrupling easy later on. With hindsight, many writers have poured scorn on such optimism, but the reason the GC

quadrupling plans came to nought was because of changing circumstances. When the London extension was planned, small-boilered 0-6-0s had worked trains of 30 to 45 wagons for many years. By the time the GC opened, 0-8-0s were moving 70 or 80 wagons trains. With larger engines, line capacity had risen, as a 70 wagon train took little more line occupancy than a 40 wagon train. This deferred the need for added capacity. The development of motor vehicles during World War One meant that a new competitor arose, further delaying any need for added line capacity. Rather than criticise the GC for their alleged failings, we should look to our own obvious lack of foresight in road building or railway regeneration today. It seems that our political masters always get it wrong today, whereas the GC would have got it right, had conditions not changed in an unforeseeable manner.

Above: It is hard to imagine a greater contrast between the gentle slopes at Rugby and the sheer-sided rock face opposite Tinsley Yard box. At the top of the rock face is an earthen bank, but even here the slope is at an acute angle, suggesting a stable formation. Given these ground conditions, there is no need for the civil engineer to cut away the ground to a gentle slope as rock excavation is costly. In deciding the appropriate type of cutting, the modeller should consider the geology of the location. The Railway Detachment of the Royal Engineers recommended a 45-degree or 1 in 1 slope for a cutting through well-drained firm earth or chalk. For shingle, gravel, dry sand or unconsolidated earth, the maximum slope should not exceed 1 in 1.5, i.e. the slope for a 20-foot deep cutting should be at least 30 foot wide. For cuttings in wet clays, the slope should be 1 in 2 to 1 in 4 depending on

conditions. The width of a 20-foot deep slope in clay would vary from 40 to 80 feet, and the overall formation for a double track line would then exceed 180 feet allowing for the tracks, the 'six-foot' between the rails, the cesses on each side and the slopes. For solid rock, the Army recommended anything up to 4 in 1, i.e. a 5-foot width for 20 feet depth, depending on the stability of the rock. On these figures, which are for military railways where speed of construction is paramount, even a shallow cutting occupies more space than we ordinarily have on our layouts. As with pointwork and curves, we may economise on space by making them more severe than is prototypical, but knowledge of the basic rules will avoid an absurd compromise. 37 095, which spent some time in the Speedlink Pool at Tinsley TMD, before going to Intercity Infrastructure at Immingham TMD, is on departmental stock.

Top: Where the railway has to cross ground that is below rail level, an embankment is necessary. The rules governing slopes of cuttings also apply to embankments, except that shrinkage and subsidence of embankments is a possibility, as materials compact down. The weight of an embankment may also cause the underlying ground to subside, so the engineer will be cautious and reduce the angle of slope. The Royal Engineers manual comments 'During the Great War attempts were made to economize time in the construction of new lines by reducing the width of cuttings and banks and widening both after the track had been laid, but they were a failure. This procedure delayed and interfered with tracklaying, and put back the date at which the lines could be used to full capacity ...When rain occurs narrow earthworks are fatal'. This embankment, near Leighton Buzzard, was photographed on 24th September 1973. The white hut and framework by the front of the AM10 unit (later class 310) were used in connection with Travelling Post Office mail

exchange apparatus on the Down Fast line. A mistake that modellers sometimes make is to put the railway boundary fencing at the top of an embankment, or the bottom of a cutting. The railway fence marks the limits of railway property and earthworks are always within the fenced area.

Above: The Settle & Carlisle Railway is one of the most spectacular lines in England. In this scenic panorama, our attention gravitates to the Class 47, but if we follow the line round beyond the train, we find that the embankment gives way to a shallow cutting as the line crosses a spur of higher ground. There is another embankment beyond this, and a deeper cutting. This succession of embankments and cuttings allows the engineer to cross difficult terrain on a reasonable grade with the minimum or earthworks. The engineer will prepare a table of quantities, listing the volume of each cutting and embankment, and if possible try to balance the two, so that he does not need to buy spoil for embankments,

or find a dumping ground for surplus material from cuttings. I recall one layout in which the modeller had introduced sweeping S bends to make it look more realistic and attractive. As there was no logical reason for his curve, it did not look realistic. Railway engineers prefer straight lines unless there is a good reason for a curve. One reason can be an ancient monument or a church that would have caused too much controversy had it been knocked down. Physical features are another possibility, as in this scene. The shortest distance from the far cutting to where we are standing would have run via the farm. Had this been the most economic route, it would have been adopted, but the ground falls away steeply beyond the farm. An even deeper and more costly embankment or viaduct would have been necessary, so the engineer used the lie of the land to minimise the earthworks. In the north of England, dry stone walls are more common than in the south, and the railway formation is enclosed by stone walls rather than wooden fencing.

Below: At Brinklow, on the Trent Valley section of the West Coast Main Line, the railway parallels the Oxford Canal. This 91 mile long waterway, which runs from Coventry to Oxford, was authorised in 1769 and opened in 1790. It predated the railway by more than half a century, and when the Trent Valley line was laid out in the 1840s, the route paralleled the canal but ran just a few feet above it. From this view of 86 210 *City of Edinburgh*, racing south with a Euston express in 1986, the railway earthworks appear to be very modest, but the canal itself is carried on a substantial embankment at this point. The combination of the narrow boats with trains makes for an eye-catching photo, and would be an attractive feature on a layout. One could envisage at least three different scenarios. One would show steam locos and narrow boats in their working life loaded with coal or other minerals. When their working career came to an end, many narrow boats were left to rot at their moorings, and around Birmingham in the 1960s, long stretches of canal had rows of partially sunken narrow boats along one bank. A layout with

sunken narrow boats, steam in its last days and first generation diesels in BR green would epitomise that era. Move forward a few years into the Rail Blue era or beyond, and the narrow boats had been raised and restored as pleasure craft.

Bottom: One of the most dramatic lengths of railway in the British Isles is the GWR line from Starcross to Teignmouth, which runs within yards of the shore. A favourite section is north of Teignmouth, where the railway shares the sea wall with the coastal walk. Brush Type 4, later Class 47, No 1714 heads an Up express towards Exeter in June 1973. This juxtaposition of towering cliffs and a railway at the foot is rare in the British Isles, though it is more common in North or South America and in parts of Europe and Asia. An American modeller, the late John Allen, was the maestro in creating stupendous cliff backdrops on his Gorre & Daphetid Railroad, but Teignmouth would make a spectacular showcase layout in a British setting. Although the construction of the railway and the sea wall have impacted on

the landscape, the red sandstone cliffs were there long before the railway, and whilst any cliffs suffer from periodic rock falls, they are a natural feature, and would look right in model or prototype form. In modelling a cliff, the vegetation at the top of the cliff will often overhang the cliff face slightly, as the loose stone or soil is eroded, but the surface material is bound to the cliff by the roots of the vegetation. Eventually the overhang becomes too great for the roots to hold, and a section collapses. The ridging of the cliffs in the distance is another characteristic feature, and is a result of water erosion.

Above: Blaenau Ffestiniog is surrounded by mountains, which tower above the town. Mankind's onslaught on these barren slate mountains turned Blaenau into one of the premier slate producing regions in the world, but created a bizarre landscape, with slate being quarried at different levels all the way up the mountain, the levels being worked by narrow gauge railways, and connected by balanced inclines. Zigzag paths were provided for the quarrymen, and the debris from quarrying spilled over the face of the mountainside. Three railways reached Blaenau. The narrow gauge Festiniog Railway was the first, arriving in the 1830s, and providing access to the sea. The GWR built a route across the mountains from Bala, whilst the LNWR built down from the North Wales coast, arriving in Blaenau Ffestiniog via a 2 mile 206 yard long tunnel that dated from 1879. All three companies opened their own stations in the town. The North Western station was a handsome gabled structure with a canopy over the approach drive. By 1974, the building was much more utilitarian, but the original boundary wall in panelled yellow brick at the north end of the buildings still survived, as did the stepped panelled wall separating the approach drive from the roadway. Given the grey roads, buildings, hillsides and even the prevailing grey weather in this part of North Wales, it provided a welcome splash of colour. The Festiniog Railway added a new exchange station adjacent to the LNWR. It was at a lower

level to the left of the station and just out of view. The only other item to relieve the ocean of grey is the yellow paintwork on the Rail Express Parcels Commer van.

Opposite page top: When railway engineers had to thread their way through large cities, they encountered constructional problems that were as challenging as any thrown up by nature, and which generated far more opposition from city dwellers. Often the only solution was an elevated route on embankments or viaducts, carrying the line high above the streets. A classic example is the North Eastern Railway at Newcastle, where the railway winds its way above the heart of the city on a succession of viaducts. The line skirts the twelfth century Keep, which overlooks the diamond junction at the east end of Newcastle Central station (see *British Railway Coaching Stock in Colour*), but turning the other way, we see the quadruple track to Manors Station, where the lines diverge to South Gosforth and Heaton. Just three quarters of a mile separates Central Station from Manors. The conduiting and cables that festoon the left hand parapet wall of the viaduct have blocked the safety refuge near the LNER 1937 electric unit. The way that brake dust and dirt have discoloured the track and the bridge parapets reveals how grimy the railway environment was. Modellers often create layouts that are a 'town planner's vision' of the ideal world, rather than realistic. The diamond crossing to the right of the unit

lacks the checkrails of a conventional diamond, as it is a switch diamond. The point motors on each side of the crossing move the blades to the through line, or for the cross over, to provide a continuous rail, avoiding the potential jolting of a diamond crossing. They also permit diamond crossovers at a finer angle than the 1 in 8 limit set by the BoT.

Opposite page bottom: As an alternative to viaducts above the city, lines can burrow beneath street level, using tunnels and sheer sided brick lined cuttings. In Birmingham, where the ground rises in the vicinity of the city centre, viaducts are used on the approach to the city from some directions, but near the centre, the lines plunge into tunnels or cuttings. Due to the topography, the approach to Birmingham New Street, the LNWR/Midland station, and the ex-GWR Snow Hill station are subterranean. In this study of light and shade, 310 062 has passed the North Tunnel junctions on the Up Stour, and is approaching platforms 6/7 in July 1976. At New Street, the platforms are split into A and B ends, so that EMUs can use both ends of the platforms, increasing line capacity considerably. The A ends are at the south of the station and the B ends at the north. Double slips or three way points are more complex and costly than simple point work, but as with a model layout, save space. It is a measure of the cramped approach to New Street that the trackwork includes a pair of double slips and a three-way point.

Railways exist to carry passengers and freight. The point where railways and their customers meet is the station. It is the focal point of activity and most modellers will want to include a station on their layout. Understanding the station is fundamental to understanding the railway, or making a layout look convincing. There are many factors that affect station design, but the most important are geographical, historical, and traffic related. In this section we shall look at the smallest stations and see what characteristic features exist, and why they take a particular form.

Top: We regard the interwar years as a time when railways started to face competition from road transport, and the closure process that led to the Beeching era began. However, there were new openings, particularly on the GWR and the Southern. From the early twenties to the end of the thirties, the GW opened dozens of new halts, at locations where changing traffic patterns offered new business. Initially served by steam railcars, they later saw auto trains, and diesel railcars. Traffic would be limited, so the extravagance of bygone days was out. Economy called for platforms of old wooden sleepers, a post and rail fence, and on double track routes, a timber pedestrian crossing, rather than a footbridge. As they were unstaffed, no booking offices were needed and the platform might be devoid of any facilities, save for a nameboard, a seat, and a couple of lamps, and even this was not universal. New Hadley, photographed on 5th July 1976, was between Oakengates and Wellington on the GW route from

Wolverhampton to Shrewsbury, and typified GWR railcar halts of the Inter-war years. Line closures, and modern Health & Safety demands for lighting have resulted in many of these small stations, including New Hadley, being closed.

Above: The Birmingham & North Warwickshire Railway started as an independent company in 1894, and was to run from a new station at Birmingham (Moor Street) to Stratford-upon-Avon. It would compete with the GWR, but came under GWR control in 1900. It was revised to run from Tyseley to Bearley Junction, where it would join the GW line from Leamington to Stratford. It opened to passengers on 1st July 1908. Good commuter services spurred residential development in Birmingham, but south of Shirley, it remained rural. Grimes Hill Platform, renamed Grimes Hill & Wythall in 1914, and later Wythall, had altered little when photographed on 9th April 1972. With a corrugated iron shelter on one

platform and a wooden shelter on the other platform, it was superior to New Hadley. Although not built under the Light Railways Act 1896, Wythall benefited from the relaxation of the rules that had guided station design for many years. BoT inspecting officers examined every new railway, every new station on existing lines, and even significant alterations, and developed a code of practice for new stations. This included raised platforms, fencing, ramps, waiting rooms on both platforms, toilets, footbridges, and clocks visible from both platforms. The requirements were reasonable for busy stations, but also applied to minor halts. By the 1880s, it was clear that a heavy outlay could not be justified on such stations, and that these rules retarded the provision of halts that might serve a few people. The Light Railways Act of 1896 recognised that a basic railway was better than no railway, and paved the way for economically built stations on other lines.

Below: Lowdham, on the Midland Railway between Nottingham to Lincoln, is more in keeping with the traditional country station. The Midland had been formed in 1844 under George Hudson's auspices. Hudson controlled the routes north from Rugby to York, but with the threat of the London & York, later the GNR, decided to build spoiling routes across the course of the proposed rival. The Nottingham & Lincoln was authorised in 1845, and was engineered by George Stephenson. It opened on 3rd August 1846. Stations displayed a variety of styles, including Classical, Tudor, and early Victorian cottage, but despite this diversity, projected an underlying 'house style' that was to characterise the Midland in later years. At Lowdham, the line crossed a minor road from Caythorpe to Lowdham village, and as was usual, this became the site for the station. The booking office, waiting room and station house were on the down platform. Openwork fretted bargeboards appeared at many Midland stations from the 1840s to the end of the nineteenth century, but the gable roof is more steeply pitched than usual. Stone mullioned windows, where stone pillars divide the glazing, were a common Midland feature, as were bay windows. In 1975, the level crossing gates, which had been re-hung on concrete posts, still survived.

Bottom: We will revisit Lowdham on 30th July 1989. Barriers controlled from a Midland Railway type 2b cabin of 1896, which still housed its original 16 lever frame, had replaced the gates. The semaphore signalling survived, as did the siding, although the goods yard closed as long ago as 15th June 1964.

Private siding traffic had survived for a time, but the reason that the yard existed 25 years after closure is because it was a useful refuge for engineers track machines. With changes to traditional infrastructure, the modeller may have to work backwards. These studies of Lowdham show what changes are likely. The gates have gone, as have the wickets. New barriers exist along with their equipment cabinets. The road crossing had been timber, but is now tarmac. The BoT requirements included ramps at the end of the platforms, to stop passengers falling off the end of the platform. The alternative, of transverse fencing, which might foul a prematurely opened carriage door, was rightly regarded as unsafe. Modern thinking is to eliminate the ramp, and put in fencing and anti-walk boarding which functions in the same way as a cow grid.

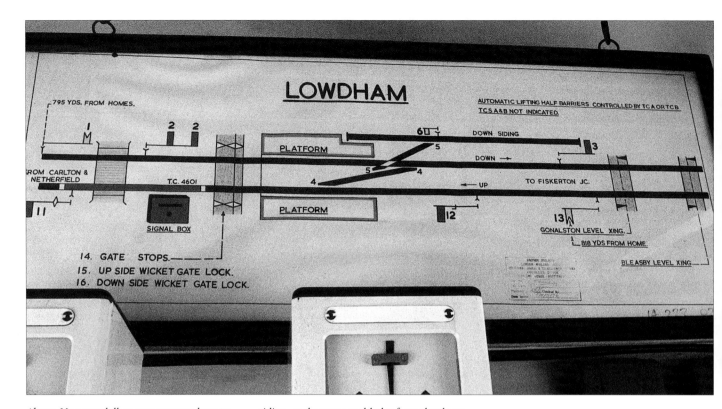

Above: Many modellers seem unsure how to signal their layouts, so I have included the signal box diagram from Lowdham. The Down main signals are Nos 1, 2 and 3. Signal No 1 is yellow with a chevron end and is the distant signal. It cannot be pulled unless 2 and 3 are also off, and tells the driver that except in emergency, he is clear through the station, and his train has been accepted by the next box, so can enter the section from Lowdham to Fiskerton Junction. If the distant is not off when the driver approaches it, he must slow down and expect to stop at the home signal, No 2. The home signal protects the level crossing and the station, and unless it has been cleared, the driver must stop here. The signal has two arms. Both arms work together, so it is co-acting. There must be sighting problems for this signal, so a top arm is provided for the driver to see at a distance, and a lower arm when the train is close to the signal. No 3 is the starting signal, and cannot be cleared until the next box has accepted the train. In the Up direction, the running signals are 11, 12 and 13. They are the Up starter, Up home and Up distant. As on the Down side, the frame is 'locked' so that No 13 cannot be pulled until 11 and 12 have been pulled. The crossover between the Up and down lines is worked by lever No 4. If No 4 is pulled to permit a move between the Up and down lines, the locking prevents the signalman clearing No 2 or 12 signals. If the Down running line signals have been pulled, and the signalman wants to shunt from the Up line to the sidings, the interlocking will stop him moving No 4 points as this would be a conflicting move. A set of points, No 5, starts part way along the crossover to provide access to the siding. This is a single slip. A train can reverse from the Up main over No 4 and No 5 into the siding, but a train cannot run from the down main into the

siding, as there are no blades from the down running line. Due to the dangers from facing points in Victorian times, access into a small wayside goods yard was always by trailing points, or a trailing crossover and single slip. On the GWR or NER shunt moves over crossovers or into sidings were normally signalled, but the MR and LNWR were more economical, reasoning that the train crew and signalman were in close proximity and could see what was intended. A small yellow signal without a fishtail arm is provided in the siding. This is NOT a distant signal, but a yellow shunt signal. Although shunt moves to the siding are not signalled, it is important that a driver should not shunt out of the siding on to the main line without a signal, so even where signalling was kept to a minimum, a signal ex the yard was common. However, the Down sidings extends along the back of the platform to a horse and carriage landing, where an end and side loading dock permitted livestock vehicles or carriage trucks to be unloaded. If the shunt signal from the yard was red, a second signal would be needed into the H+C landing, as the driver must NOT pass a red signal. This would be a needless complication. The answer was a yellow ground signal. If the driver is going into the H+C landing, he may pass it at danger. It is only if he is going out on to the main line that it needs to be cleared. The diagram shows that automatic half barriers have been installed at Gonalston and Bleasby level crossings. No 14 is the gate stop. When the gates are closed against the road, and clear for the railway, this locks them in position. It is interlocked with the home signals for added safety. Wicket gates are the small gates for foot passengers. As the train is approaching the signalman pulls these levers locking the wickets and preventing a pedestrian rushing in front of the train.

Opposite page top: Lenwade is a small community in Norfolk northwest of Norwich, and from 1882 until 1959, was on the Lynn & Fakenham, later Midland & Great Northern Railway, route from Melton Constable to Norwich City. The line opened from Melton to Lenwade on 1st July 1882, trains reaching Norwich on 2nd November 1882. After closure to passengers, Lenwade handled general freight until 31st October 1966, and traffic for the Anglian Building products private sidings into the 1970s. The M&GNJR was an amalgam of several companies, and traversed North Norfolk, an area that was otherwise a GER monopoly. It was owned jointly by the Midland Railway and the GNR, both appointing directors. Because of this dual control, much of its rolling stock and infrastructure was provided by the parent companies, so one might see a GN-designed locomotive next to Midland signal box or vice versa. The long serving chief engineer to 'The Joint', William Marriott, was a fine engineer who accepted GN or Midland expertise where it was beneficial, but from 1896, an M&GN style began to evolve. Lenwade had a Lynn & Fakenham Railway box on the platform when opened in 1882, but the layout was altered in 1899, and an M&GN type 1b signal box, to a design that was current from 1903 to 1916, appeared later. Unlike Lowdham, where the MR gates had been replaced by LNWR-style gates with horizontal tie rods, the crossing gates at Lenwade are standard Midland gates, with ⅜in vertical iron bars, and are an example of how the parent companies supplied standard equipment to 'The Joint'. The gate timbers are secured to the hinge straps by five bolts, whilst the end straps have just four bolts.

Above: Lenwade box, taken on 13th July 1971, shows that this apparently all timber box is actually formed of concrete blocks up to waist height. William Marriott, the M&GN chief engineer, knew that the base is liable to rot in a wooden box, and as an early exponent of concrete, designed and installed concrete block making equipment at Melton Constable works. Sleepers, buildings and signal posts were turned out in concrete. The space below the operating floor houses the locking. A door is usually provided at one end, and there may be small windows on the front. End windows are rare, and the large end windows of the Marriott type 1b box are unusual. The Norwich line was single, and although there was no passing loop at Lenwade, it was a block post. Trains could not pass at Lenwade, so they would not be accepted from both directions, unless one was a freight to work into the yard, but such block posts were common on 'The Joint', permitting a frequent service in the same direction. On a line with heavy summer traffic, where traffic would flow one way at certain times of day and the other way later on, this was a cheap way to increase line capacity. The M&GN lattice paling fence was characteristic of 'The Joint'.

Top right: At some stations, the stationmaster's house was combined with the station building, in which case a two-storey structure was normal. Where the station house was separate, a single story building sufficed. Although the original Lynn & Fakenham Railway signal box at Lenwade had been replaced, the L&F booking office and waiting room of 1882 survived throughout the station's life. A similar building, with ornate bargeboards on the gables was provided at Hindolvestone at the Melton end of the Norwich line. Indeed the two stations were almost identical, and in both cases, the signal box was on the platform just feet from the station building. After a new box was provided at Lenwade, the site of the original L&F cabin was occupied by the more modern Marriott-designed concrete block goods warehouse visible to the right of the buildings. It was often possible to trace the evolution of a station, and of its traffic, by means of features dating from different periods. Where a particularly strong minded and innovative officer held sway for some years, the process could be particularly informative and interesting. Marriott was one such character, but sadly little of his railway has survived.

Right: The L&F was unusual for its architectural harmony when built. The station buildings, the original signal box and the goods shed all shared the same pattern of bargeboards. Unusually, wagons did not work into the goods shed, but were positioned alongside two pairs of opening doors, and merchandise was transferred between the wagon and the shed. Although offering less protection to goods in inclement weather, this permitted a smaller and cheaper structure. The red and white 'Harlequin' sign on the end of the building is a 'Limited Clearance' sign, which was used widely by BR to warn staff when it was unsafe to pass alongside a structure if vehicle movements were to take place. Although the station was painted in Eastern Region colours in BR days, traces of a chocolate brown shade are visible where paint is flaking off the bargeboard. The M&GN painted its buildings in a milk chocolate brown and cream, and from inspecting M&GN structures that survived at the start of the 1970s, it is clear that brown paint was widely applied to bargeboards, and in the case of timber buildings, to the framework as well. Strakes on the ornamental fretwork of platform canopies were picked out alternately brown and cream.

Opposite page top: Gorey is on the Dublin, Wicklow & Wexford (later the Dublin & South Eastern Railway) main line that runs south from Dublin along the Irish coast, connecting its name towns. Although a main line, most of the route has always been single track, and Gorey is a small but fascinating station. The signal box, which is the green structure on the down platform, is carried on stilts, as was common with signal boxes erected up to the 1860s. The point rodding is fully exposed, but the box actually dates from as late as 1891, so the design is a remarkable throwback to early times. Detailed views of the cabin appeared in *British Railway Signalling in Colour*. The DW&W was always hard up, and to save money on building separate steps up to the box, the signalman entered from the adjacent passenger footbridge. This was exceptional in England, but is encountered in Ireland. The starter from the down platform is visible against the sky just below the footbridge. The right hand platform is bi-directionally signalled, and the red arm of the starter is visible to the right of the bridge opening. Until the partition of Ireland in the 1920s, Irish railways came under the United Kingdom Board of Trade, so BoT rules over facing points applied, but at stations on single lines where bi-directional lines exist, any connection off the bi-directional track will be facing for trains in one direction. The points in the foreground, No 10, are into the yard.

Above: Irish Rail's General Motors diesel No 162 has arrived with a freight train from the south, and is shunting cement wagons over No 10 crossover. On passenger lines, the Board of Trade required any facing points to be locked, so that they could not be accidentally moved by the signalman under a passing train. These principles became so engrained in the minds of professional railwaymen, that they have endured long after BoT control of the railways of Ireland ceased. Locking could be achieved by a point lever and a separate locking lever, but to save levers, an 'economical facing point lock' was developed whereby the point lever also worked the locking bar. This is a long metal bar that is placed inside one running rail just before the point, and is pivoted on cranks so it can be raised or lowered. The locking bar is beside the far rail just behind the rearmost wagon. When the signalman pulls the lever, the first thing to happen is that the locking bar is lifted up by the cranks, so that its' face is level with the head of the rail. If the track is unoccupied, the bar can be raised, the point blades can then be moved, and as the lever completes its stroke, the bar returns to the normal position. If a vehicle is standing on the locking bar when the signalman attempts to pull the lever, the flanges of the wheels will prevent the signalman raising the locking bar, so it will not be possible to continue the lever movement. The way the point blades are set cannot be altered, and an accident is averted. It is a simple idea, but with the spread of track circuiting and power box working, the same function is achieved electrically.

PLATFORM FURNITURE

Above: Black and white photographs of pre-grouping stations show a profusion of signs. They were large, with upper case letters for clarity. Although railwaymen had not attended design school, they realised from experience what stood out and what did not, and acted accordingly. To provide even greater clarity, and to help the illiterate, vital signs, such as the

'WAY OUT' were fitted with a pointing hand. This tradition endured on the railways until the 1960s when 'design' became the buzzword. Corporate image was in, and pointing hands were old fashioned. The new signs were modern looking, much smaller, and used fashionable lower case lettering, because the designers, rather than being practical men, had attended design courses. The signs were hard to read from the platform, and it was even worse if you were looking from your carriage window as the train entered the station, but they were modern, and that is what counted. A

wholesale resigning of stations took place, and everyone lived happily ever after. For some reason, the citizens of Hebden Bridge were denied this benefit, and their station, which had been rebuilt by the Lancashire & Yorkshire Railway about 1909, benefited little from the new standards. Eventually the station buildings with their glazed canopy, and the wooden signs, were declared a Grade II listed building, denying for ever the benefits of unreadable modern signs to the inhabitants of Hebden Bridge as this 1990 portrait reveals.

Left: Ancaster has a population of around 500 to 600 people, and is in Lincolnshire, 8 miles from Grantham and 6 miles from Sleaford. It is on the Great Northern line from Nottingham to Boston. The section from Barkston, near Grantham, to Sleaford, opened on 16th June 1857. Initially it was leased to the GNR, but was absorbed by the Great Northern in 1864. This comparison of a GNR running-in board at Ancaster, and its corporate image rival, is a graphic commentary on the wisdom and sense of different generations. The lettering of the GNR 'running in' board, which is of cast iron and supported on concrete posts, is raised for greater clarity, and is easy to repaint periodically. The play of light and shadow makes for an attractive image, but to suggest this is chance would be wrong. It is good design. The board is elegantly framed, and whilst the framework adds to the appearance, it contributes to strength and durability. The posts, which are topped with ball finials, are robust and long lasting, whilst the shaped brackets that help support the board are evidence of practical attention to detail. When photographed on 4th July 1989, it had seen many decades of service. Its corporate image neighbour is fading and looking shabby. Without raised letters as a guide, repainting is not practicable, so it must be replaced. The purpose of a sign is to give information. Even in ideal lighting, it cannot compare with its predecessor, and at dusk or by night it is far worse. Logic tells us that as we gain experience, things should improve, yet this illustration reveals the opposite.

Right: Although some writers have castigated the early days of BR as lacking clarity of vision, the reverse is true. Rather than the depressing anonymity of corporate image, management knew that company loyalties could be harnessed in the same way that the army harnesses regimental pride. The clearest example was the adoption of regional colours, coupled with a nationwide policy over signing. The colours were well chosen, and with the exception of the Dark Blue for the Eastern, and Orange for the North Eastern Regions, had company or national affinities. They were brown for the Western Region, green for the Southern, red for the London Midland and Light Blue for Scotland. Although enamelled steel signs supplanted raised letters, the quality of manufacture was high, and the use of the largest practicable size of upper case characters made for clarity. Although I prefer GWR station signs, this 'running-in' board at Stourbridge Junction, which reuses the old GWR support posts, must score highly. The colour contrast is good; it projects a national image, yet boosts regional pride. The letters are large, so it is easy to read, and when photographed on 2nd July 1976, it had stood the test of time. The unit, which comprises 50340, a Gloucester RCW class 100 car of 1957, and 50497, a BRCW class 104/1 car, is stabled at the far end of the Stourbridge Town platform. With the decline in the numbers of station staff, weeds have flourished, as this section of the platform is no longer in regular public use.

Below: The North Eastern Region colours of tangerine (orange) and white, although having no direct connections with the LNER, were striking. Today, Grosmont is best known as the northern terminus of the North Yorkshire Moors Railway, but it is still on the national network as well, on the NER line from Middlesbrough to Battersby Junction and Whitby. Back in July 1974, the NYMR was still in its infancy, and regional colours survived on the BR section of the station where the sign, the platform lamps and even the shelter carried orange paint. The nameboard on the signal cabin was also in regional colours. Grosmont box, an unusual overhung NE cabin on a narrow base, which dated from 1904, was moved to Slaggyford after it became redundant for BR purposes. Instead of the wooden platform fencing which was common in the south, a robust stone wall edges the platform. Attention to company or regional details helps define and locate a layout. The platform is on a tight curve, and BoT regulations for passenger lines provided that where the radius was under 10 chains, the curve had to be continuously check railed. The checkrail is visible on the inside of the left hand rail.

Top: Alresford is now on the preserved Mid Hants Railway which runs from there to Alton, but on 27th July 1972, it was a sleepy wayside station on the former London & South Western Railway branch from Winchester to Alton. The threat of closure had hung over the line ever since the publication of the Beeching Report on the reshaping of British Railways in 1963. According to Beeching, any route that carried less than 10,000 passengers a week was uneconomic, and the Winchester to Alton line, which failed that test, was eking out its last months of life prior to closure in 1973. The green paintwork on lamps and barrows, which had been a feature since Southern days, and was continued by BR, was faded, and the gas lamps, carried on their barley twist standards (so named from their alleged similarity to a barley stick), looked tired, as did the Southern luggage trolleys parked near the canopy. These giant trolleys, some of which had spoked wheels, whilst others sported disc wheels, were a feature of the Southern and unlike anything on the rest of BR. The combination of white, green and cream paint, which was adopted by the Southern Region, copied Southern Railway practice, and at times it was hard to know if one was looking at BR livery or well-worn Southern paintwork. The narrow bicycle shed, with the bikes standing almost upright was another Southern feature, as was the concrete panel fencing between the station buildings and the signal box. The box dated from c1875, and was to the LSWR type 1 pattern. When new, it was externally framed, that is, the structural timbers were visible outside a single layer of planking, but in common with most type 1 boxes, it later received an additional external cladding. Rather than lapped weatherboarding, it was clad in sheet timber. The decorative valance above the windows was once common on type 1 boxes, but it was probably the last box to retain this attractive feature.

Left: The type 210 barrow was the Midland counterpart to the big LSWR/Southern barrows. No Midland station was complete without one, but when I photographed this example at Nottingham Midland on 6th July 1976, they were fast disappearing under the onslaught of the BR 'Brute' trolleys. This is a late example, with spoked rather than disc wheels, whilst the middle of the three horizontal end bars overlaps the verticals. They were six feet long, with a width of two feet. They had probably been turned out in crimson lake ever since Midland days. Tare weight was commonly given, and the station to which they were allocated might also appear.

Above: Apart from the two-wheel barrow, most stations had four wheeled platform trolleys. As with the Midland type 210 barrow, some had spoked wheels, whilst others had disc wheels with strengthening ribs and holes. Both types appear on platform 2 at Crewe about 1976. Trolleys had a hinged towing handle at one end, which was surmounted by a heart shaped handgrip or a T piece. When the trolley was not in use, the handle rested at an angle against the bed. To move the trolley, the porter swung the handle forward, and because the leading axle was pivoted, and the handle was attached to it by a projecting bar, it was easy to move the trolley in any direction. On some designs, the handle was connected to a brake. When the handle rested against the bed, the brake gripped the wheel. When the porter moved the handle forward, the brake was pulled off. This was a valuable safety precaution, as it prevented accidents such as the Wellingborough derailment of 2nd September 1898 when a trolley that had been left unattended, rolled on to the track in front of an express, causing the engine and train to derail, with a loss of seven lives. Had the trolley been fitted with an automatic brake, the accident could not have happened. Another design lacked an automatic brake, but had a steel scotch that hung down from a hook when out of use, but could be pushed against the wheel. The maroon trolley is to this design. Battery powered trolleys that could tow slave trolleys appeared in the 1920s. The yellow painted Post Office trolley is a slave trolley with automatic brakes. In the distance are some blue BR 'Brutes' (British Railways Universal Transport Equipment) trolleys. The profusion of conduiting on the platform face and to the right of the footbridge merits study.

Below: From the 1830s until January 2004, the General Post Office and its successors were extensive users of the railways, sorting mail on Travelling Post Office trains, and moving parcels by rail. A gaggle of Post Office trolleys await their next duty at Newark Castle station on 3rd July 1989. One has plain disc wheels. The other has disc wheels with ribs and holes. One has end supports, so it can be loaded with tiers of mail sacks. The other has open ends. So that rainwater will drain away, these Post Office trolleys have widely spaced slats, as is evident from the pattern of light and shade on the platform. Railway trolleys generally had a solid decking. The Midland Railway station buildings date from the opening of the station in 1846, were in a mildly classical style, with unusual curved ends, and were constructed in a creamy-yellow 'buff' brick.

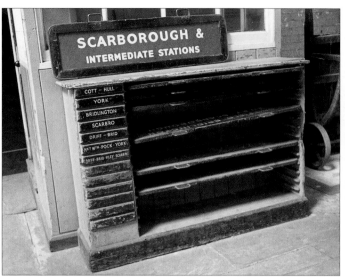

were lockable, the stationmasters having a key to the short flap, but only the district office having the key to the long flap. The stationmaster unlocked the short flap, and raised it up. As he did so, a second flap, that was rigidly attached to it at an angle, appeared. This second flap was longer that the top flap, so it would jam against the side of the box. The stationmaster could drop his pouch on this flap, but it prevented him reaching into the safe. When he dropped the flap, the pouch fell into the box, and could not be retrieved. In some designs, when the flap was dropped it locked automatically. At the district offices, the safe was taken to the cash office, where the long flap was unlocked in the presence of two members of staff. Unlike the short flap with a second angled lid, this was a single flap, and permitted access to the box. The long flap was opened, the pouches removed and their contents checked. The night safe at a bank works on a similar principle. Box No 26, which was used between Wellington and the Wolverhampton Division offices, is awaiting collection by train at Wellington on the afternoon of 30th June 1976.

Above: The BoT requirements covered fundamental safety issues and quite trivial matters of passenger convenience. In the nineteenth century, a watch was a luxury item that was beyond the purse of the working man. To remedy this, the BoT insisted that railway companies should provide clocks that were visible from the platform. Some of the best-known examples, such as the clock at Waterloo, hung high above the concourse, but most clocks faced the platform. The drumhead clock, so called because it was the size and shape of a drum, with the mechanism contained in its drum-like body, was usual, but this attractive long case clock was photographed at Maidstone West on 10th June 1973. The provision of a lamp that shines directly on the clock is indicative of how seriously railwaymen took the provision of accurate time to their passengers and staff.

Above right: In the days before electronic displays, the provision of time and destination data had to be done manually. One method was to use a frame into which destination boards were inserted. When not in use, the boards were stored in a rack. The NER rack at Beverley still survived in July 1974. One board has been placed on top of the rack to demonstrate their appearance. When not in use it would be pushed into the fourth slot from the top, which carried a plate SCAR'BRO. The Driffield, Bridlington, Filey, Scarborough board is not only in the wrong slot, it is not even in the same slot at opposite ends of the rack. Below the painted boards are 'blackboards' which receive chalked descriptions for special workings, the uppermost blackboard in fact bearing a chalked inscription 'special'.

Bottom right: Railways needed to transfer cash and daily returns from stations to district offices. The answer was to put them in a pouch and send them by train, but if cash was entrusted to the guard, it was placing temptation in his way. The solution was the travelling safe. This was a wooden box with iron framing and lifting handles. Some safes operated from one station to a district office, but others picked up returns from several stations en route. Each station needed to put their pouches in the safe, but should not be able to remove any other pouches. The travelling safe had a two-part lid that was hinged off centre. Both flaps

Right: Station seats were as diverse as any aspect of railway infrastructure, and help fix a location. The GWR preferred cast seat ends with the initials on display. The Furness Railway incorporated a squirrel in the seat ends. Predictably, the LNWR was economical, using strip steel bent into a suitable shape, but the wooden backrest had a sausage shaped rebate to which cast iron letters were screwed giving the station name. In many cases, such as Rugby or Crewe, the name was short, but at Nuneaton, the existence of the competing Midland Station induced the company to emblazon NUNEATON TRENT VALLEY along the backrest. This was a very familiar seat to Clive Partridge, who has guided me in many technical details, and was in this condition when he took charge of Nuneaton. He decided to smarten up the station, and had the seats repainted in maroon with the lettering picked out in white. The appearance of shaped perforated steel seats at many stations in recent years is an understandable response to vandalism, but lacks the charm of yesteryear.

Below: From the dawn of the railway age poster boards were provided at stations. This modern example was photographed at Thorne North, at the southern extremity of the NER near Goole, shows a colourful South Yorkshire PTE/BR timetable and an attractive East Coast Main Line electrification poster. As with seats, items such as this help locate and date a railway, for the photograph was taken on 7th August 1989, and refers to the target date for completion of electrification to Edinburgh in May 1991. Traces of earlier posters peep out below or to the right. Poster boards, such as these, would add credibility to a layout, in the larger scales at least.

Bottom right: The least welcome poster was headed 'BRITISH RAILWAYS BOARD, TRANSPORT ACT 1962, PROPOSAL TO DISCONTINUE RAILWAY PASSENGER SERVICES'. Its appearance heralded the start of a process that was created to facilitate closure, whilst preserving a veneer of public accountability. The name of the Transport Users' Consultative Committee, with its inference that users would be consulted, was calculated to inspire confidence, but within a few years, those who found their local stations threatened realised it was a toothless tiger. Many lines that were closed as a result of the Beeching Report had no

were obliged to operate. Many closures were in the national interest, but others were obtained by an inexcusable system, which should have received the discredit it richly warranted, had the TUCC chairmen not adopted a 'Pontius Pilate' act. With a balanced closure process, lines that were useless would have been shed, but valuable lines would have survived. By the time the closure of Gainsborough Central, Kirton Lindsay and Brigg was proposed in 1989, politicians had become aware of the sensitivity of rail closures, and protesters were more politically aware, so the objectors invariably won, as in this case.

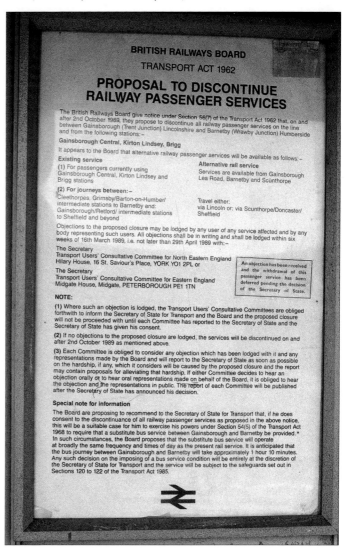

role to play in the age of motor transport, but once a rationalisation mentality gripped BR, divisional officers vied with one another to show who was best at 'rationalisation', and if the overall results suggested that a closure was of doubtful wisdom, data would be massaged to guarantee 'success'. On the Hunstanton branch, for example, a traffic census of receipts from branch stations was conducted in mid winter. As the main traffic was in summer from London and other towns to the seaside, the results were not a fair representation of the traffic on the line, but the TUCC was legally debarred from questioning such data. Rather than going along with this farce, which was intended to confer respectability on the closure proposals, TUCC chairman should have prefaced their reports with a clear statement of the glaring faults in the system they

Above: The Victorians, as modern writers tell us, had many faults. They also had many virtues, and realised that men and horses might feel thirsty when they were about their daily business. The nascent animal welfare lobby took steps to quench the thirst of horses, whilst it was the Temperance Movement that took the lead in quenching the thirst of men, as a thirsty man might be lured to damnation in a public house, if he could not find more wholesome refreshment. Drinking fountains which were paid for by the Temperance Movement or erected through their lobbying, appeared in a myriad of places, so that the thirsty man had little need at any hour of the day or night to risk eternal damnation. Between 1883 and 1886, the LNWR completely remodelled Rugby station, sweeping away the old and inadequate 1840s structure, and building a magnificent island platform with plentiful facilities. The station was completed in 1886, but a marble drinking fountain had been provided the previous year. It survived in March 2000, though the water supply had been turned off and the bowl was used as a flowerbed.

Above left: Though modern men might have to risk damnation at Rugby, with the demise of the public drinking water supply, Virgin Trains have inherited the British love of animals, and a dog's drinking bowl has been provided. Literate dogs would read the inscription, 'Please quench your thirst with our best wishes', whilst less educated canines, would know that the yellow poodle indicated a drinking stand, just as humans recognise the international signs for ladies or gents. This is the most modern piece of infrastructure in this book, and Virgin are to be congratulated for the spirit in which it has been done, and the humour as well.

Top: Safety has long been a major consideration on the railways, and until recent years, a row of red painted buckets, often with a black base and handle, existed at most stations. Prominently lettered FIRE, and kept filled with water, their use could prevent a trivial fire becoming a major conflagration. As they were good quality metal buckets, theft, including the acquisition of buckets that carried such hallowed letters as GWR by enthusiasts, has eradicated them from the station scene. Indeed one bucket is missing from this display at Chorley Wood on 14th August 1989. Chorley Wood is on the Metropolitan & GC Joint Railway, and carries main line and London Underground (Metropolitan) services. The Met & GC Joint was a strange alliance that took the Metropolitan Railway to the remote country lanes of Buckinghamshire, and the Great Central into the heart of London. Chorley Wood signal box, visible in the distance, is a Metropolitan Railway type 1 box dating from 1889. It survived in permanent way use after its signalling career ended.

MEDIUM SIZED STATIONS

My classification of Small, Medium or Large stations is unofficial. Under 'Small Stations', we looked at locations with one or two platforms, simple buildings and minimal freight facilities. In this section we will explore stations with more potential. Traditionally, the coverage of stations is confined to the station frontage or the platforms, so it is difficult for the modeller to know what the rest of the station looks like. Rather than fall into the trap of showing less by showing more, I have covered three stations. You may not want to model these stations, but the relationship of the various features will help the modeller to understand other locations.

Right: Bude is a seaside resort on the north coast of Cornwall. For many years, it was served by the Atlantic Coast Express, that astonishing train that left Waterloo, and shed portions for all the seaside resorts on the former LSWR lines in Devon and Cornwall. . Sadly, Bude fell victim to a twin onslaught. First of all, the BR traffic survey of April 1961, showed less than 5,000 passengers a week, as well it might out of season. That was ample to condemn it, but the Southern lines west of Exeter were transferred to Western Region control from 1st January 1963, and that guaranteed its fate. Although railway rivalry was understandable, and a spirit of competition between the regions was sound, the record on 'penetrating' lines that were transferred from their parent region to new control was poor. No region escapes blame, but the Western

Region's behaviour was probably the worst of all BR regions. It is hard to look back on WR control of the Southern lines west of Exeter without concluding that destruction of a one time rival was paramount. The Bude branch did not open until 11th August 1898, making it one of the last holiday resorts to get on the railway map. The signal box, which was photographed in July 1966, was an LSWR type 4 box. This design originated in 1894-95, and was continued by the Southern until about 1928. Unlike most boxes, where continuous glazing was provided at the front, these boxes had a brick pillar at the centre and shallow windows. Alternate windows could slide, so no cleaning walkway was required. It was a plain, and economical design with low maintenance costs. A few survive, but not Bude, as the station closed to passengers on 3rd October 1966. Given the small resident population and the limited winter traffic, closure was justified, but the dubious tricks played elsewhere, and the delight that the WR took in destroying its

Southern conquests, have left a legacy of suspicion. Before natural gas from the North Sea, most towns had their local gas works, and despite just 5,000 people in Bude in the 1950s, the gas works was sizeable. It was served by a coal chute on the quay branch, which curves away from the station behind the box.

Bottom: At Bude, the signalman would have seen the locomotive shed, the water tank, a run round loop, a platform with two faces, the canopy and station building, end-loading, side-loading, cattle dock facilities and a brick built goods shed. Watering facilities exist on the platform and by the shed. The rail built bracket signal in the centre of the view controls departures from the two platforms. It is placed an engine length beyond the platforms, as this permits the full length of the platform to be occupied by passenger stock, the engine sitting beyond the end of the platform, but within the protection of the signal.

Top: Beverley is a market town of around 16,000 people in the East Riding of Yorkshire. It is best known for its Minster, which is on a site that has been in religious use since the eighth century, though the present Minster dates from the thirteenth to fifteenth centuries. It houses a fourteenth century shrine to the Percys, the great baronial lords of the north. Our reason for visiting Beverley on 9th July 1974 was to see the Minster, but Beverley station was also on our itinerary. The station was designed by George Townsend Andrews, a close friend of 'The Railway King', George Hudson. An architect and High Sheriff of York, Andrews was well placed to help Hudson, and in return, received the contracts for many stations on his railways. This advanced his career, but Andrews was an exceptionally talented architect, and was to create many fine structures. Beverley station was on the Bridlington extension of the Hull & Selby Railway. This line, authorised under acts of 1843 and 1845, ran north from Hull to Driffield, and then turned north-east to reach the sea at Bridlington. It was leased to Hudson's York & North Midland Railway in 1845, and opened on 6th October 1846. The

frontage of Beverley station was a single story brick building in neo-classical style with dressed stone quoins at the end of the buildings, and a cornice, which is the projecting stone moulding just below roof level, supported on a row of dentils, the projecting stone blocks. A glazed canopy, supported on cast iron spandrels, completed the ensemble.

Above: The exterior was pleasant, but what made Beverley exceptional was the train shed. In the early days, many engineers, including Brunel, favoured train sheds at intermediate stations. With the growth of the rail network and station enlargements, many were swept away during station remodellings, but in 1945, eight survived at former York & North Midland stations in the East Riding. By the 1970s, closures or retrenchment had reduced this to three, of which that at Beverley was the most imposing. Brick walls supported an iron-trussed hipped roof with plentiful glazing panels to provide a light and airy interior. With a wooden train shed, the tie beams are horizontal throughout their length. With iron framed roofs, the tie rod usually consists of two

lengths of 'T' iron that rise by about ¹⁄₄₀ of the width of the span to the centre point, or as at Beverly, a truss where the tie rod is in three sections, the outer sections sloping up gently to a horizontal middle portion, the rise being about ¹⁄₅₀ of the span. In such a roof, a strut runs from the point where the angle of the tie rod changes to the principal roof beam, joining the latter at right angles. This strut and the principal are in compression. The tie rod and the strut that runs diagonally to the apex of the roof are in tension. The additional struts provide further strength to a long span. In this view, taken on 9th July 1974, we are looking towards Hull, with the footbridge, newsagents stall, station entrance, ticket collectors booth and the rack for destination boards visible from left to right. The clock is on a V shaped frame with faces pointing up and down the line, and is visible from both platforms, meeting the BoT requirements. NER station seats with splayed rusticated legs, two platform barrows which are probably to NER diagram 60, and three diagram 62 or 63 platform trolleys with 'T' handles, complete an essentially pre-grouping scene that was taken half a century after the company lost its identity.

Right: Many important NER stations, including Beverley, received a tiled system map. The map tiles were 8 x 8 in, with some half-height tiles bearing the heading 'NORTH EASTERN RAILWAY'. They were enclosed in a brown border that was about 3in depth, giving an overall size of 70 x 75in for the tiled map. We photographed the map 'square on' with a view to reducing it to a suitable size for modelling, but lacking an NER station, have never been able to use it on our own layout. NER modellers are most welcome to copy it to reduced size for inclusion on their own layouts. In OO scale, it will be approximately 1in square, so would make an attractive feature.

Below: The ornamental wooden valance at the end of the train shed is horizontal, but the footbridge is a graceful arch, springing from platform level, and creating an attractive frame for Beverley Minster. Passengers have been able to see the towers of the Minster soaring up into the sky for almost 160 years, but it is a sobering thought that the towers at the west end date from 1390 – 1420, so were more than 400 years old when the railway came to Beverley. At the time when the Hull & Bridlington line was built, railways were either welcomed or opposed on principle. Level crossings were not seen as a major problem, as road traffic was light and trains infrequent. At Beverley, the line crossed four roads on the level within a few hundred yards. The first was Flemingate, a quarter of a mile south of the station. The second crossing, worked by the station box was just short of the station. The third crossing, over Cherry Tree Lane, was half a mile north of the station, and the final crossing was controlled by Beverley North box.

Top: We are looking towards Bridlington on 9th July 1974 as 20 130 approaches with a mixed freight from Beverley to Hull. The graceful arch of the footbridge, which is to the 1891 NER standard pattern, complements the train shed to produce a striking composition. The stairways from the footbridge pierce the glazed end screens to the train shed, whilst the base of the footbridge is bricked in, with a door facing the track. This reduces the draughtiness of the platform and provides a storage area as well. The glazed screen at the far end of the train shed is not pierced by

stairs, so is clearly visible, as is the flat valance, as it is not obscured by the arch of the footbridge.

Above: The lever frame of Beverley Station box helps explain the later scenes. It is a 1911 NER Southern Division type 4 box, and housed a 36 lever McKenzie & Holland frame, later reduced to 20 levers, but even in 1974, I wonder how much of the original frame survived, as many replacement parts had been supplied by the Westinghouse Brake & Saxby Co to McKenzie & Holland design. Red levers 2, 3 and 4 are the

Up running signals. Surprisingly the distant is No 6. The likely reason is that with mechanical signals at a considerable distance, it will be a heavy 'pull', and No 1 lever is very close to the end of the box, cramping the signalman's ability to throw all his weight into the pull. No 9 is a shunt signal setting back over points 10, the trailing crossover at the north end of the station, or setting back along the down main. The red, black, red group, 14 to 16 are for the points out of the Up sidings and the respective signals. No 16 also controls setting back movements over No 10. No 18 is an elevated ground signal from the down platform over crossover 22, which is south of the box, and is provided with a facing point lock, No 21. No 23 is the release lever for the next crossing box to the south at Flemingate. No 28 permits set back moves over 22 points, whilst the black and white chevrons on No 29 show it works a detonator placer. Upwards chevrons were for the Up line, and downwards chevrons for the Down line. Nos 30 to 32 are the Down running signals and 33 is the Down distant. On levers 32 and 33, the tops of the handles have been cut off. Mechanical signals and points can be a heavy pull, and the signalman needs to use all his strength to throw the levers. Electrically worked signals or colour lights can be flicked over with little effort, and a signalman could be injured if he applied all his strength to move such a lever. To prevent this, the lever tops are cut short. Nos 34 and 35 control the pedestrian wicket gates at the crossing, and No 36 is the gate lock, interlocking the gates and signals.

Above: Freight facilities existed on both sides of the line at the north of the station, and extended across Cherry Tree Lane crossing, which is visible beyond the class 20 in the yard. Shunt signal 16, which is in the 'six foot' between the running lines, is 'led' by the trailing crossover from the Up to the down line, lever No 10, or by crossover to the Up Goods Independent on the right hand side of the line. The word 'led' means that lever 16 could not be pulled unless 10 or 15 points had been pulled previously. This would prevent a wrong direction setting back movements along the Up main towards Cherry Tree. However, the LNER local instructions did permit right-direction propelling movements on the down line from Beverley station to Cherry Tree and over the level crossing to Beverley North box. These boxes were in close proximity, so the platform starter, lever No 30 at the station box, was 'slotted' i.e. shared with Cherry Tree box, and was also his down home signal. To clear the signal, the station box would offer the train to Cherry Tree, who would accept it, but for the arm to come off, both signalmen would have to pull the levers in their boxes. The distant arm beneath No 30 is the outer distant for Beverley North box. It will only come off if Beverley North has offered the train to the next box and had it accepted, and the Station box and Cherry Tree pull the platform starter, and Beverley North pulls all his signals including the distant! A signal post stands between Cherry Tree box and the class 20. This lower arm is Beverley North's inner distant. The use

of outer and inner distants is required when boxes are in close proximity, and braking distance from the inner distant, in this case the signal near the class 20, is insufficient, so another distant is required under the previous stop signal. The cranked post signal to the right of the Up Main is Beverley station's home signal No 2.

Below: Cherry Tree box, half a mile north of the station box, worked Cherry Tree Lane crossing and controlled the connections into the down yard. As there was only a short distance between the station and Cherry Tree Lane, the yard points spread out just south of the road, and the yard headshunt crossed the

road behind the box. Before a shunt move, the signalman had to close the crossing to road users, which must have delighted motorists! Cherry Tree was an NER Southern Division type S4 box. A brick base with tubular steel handrails has replaced the original timber staircase. We have used eight views to explore Beverley, as we have an 1840s station with an overall trainshed, four level crossings, a goods yard, and an independent freight line. At Beverley North, a long abandoned branch line turned west towards York. It is a complex pattern, but one that covers an astonishing range of railway infrastructure, and shows how a railway had to weave its way through a pre-existing urban environment.

Left: Newtown, on the Cambrian line between Welshpool and Dovey Junction, is located in Montgomeryshire, and its nearest neighbour to the north is Abermule, a station that achieved notoriety due to the fateful head-on collision in 1921. With a population of just 5,600 in the 1950s, Newtown is a small community, but given the slight population of central Wales, it is important in a local context. The Beeching Report revealed that fewer than 10,000 passengers used the line each week, but political factors, and poor roads in Central Wales, persuaded Beeching not to wield his axe this time. The Llanidloes & Newtown Railway was authorised in 1853, and opened to passengers on 2nd September 1859. Until the completion of the 30 mile long Oswestry & Newtown Railway on 10th June 1861, through freight continued by canal, as the L&N was isolated from the rest of the rail network. Extension to the coast was by the Newtown & Machynlleth Railway, which left the L&N at Moat Lane Junction, and opened in 1863. All these impoverished companies became part of the equally impoverished Cambrian Railways. The original station at Newtown was abysmal, and a protest campaign led to a promise by the Cambrian Railways in October 1868 to rebuild the station. The line ran on a shelf cut in the sloping hillside south of the town centre, and a flight of steps led from the station forecourt to an attractive porch with a pointed arch, a pyramid shaped finial, and trefoil and quatrefoil openings in the bargeboards. The unusual combination of plain columns with acanthus leaf capitals supporting the arch, and an ecclesiastical theme to the door panelling, produced a diverse effect. The blackboard, promoting special cheap day returns on Sundays was a traditional aspect of railway advertising, depending for its effect upon local artistic skill and enthusiasm.

Below: On 27th August 1973, Newtown station retained a strong Cambrian/Great Western atmosphere. Mail bags lie at the far end of the open shelter on the down platform, whilst the complex roof finials, and ecclesiastical tone of the door panelling, repeat the themes already encountered on the porch. The extraordinary wooden supports to the canopy merit attention. Even without the chocolate and cream GENTLEMEN sign, the louvred ventilator on the end wall proclaims a toilet. As the ladies toilet was usually reached off the Ladies Waiting Room, rather than from an end door, this is likely to be the gents. With the closure of many station toilets, observation of such details helps us to work out what a building might have been like. At the far end of the platform is a GWR 'running in' board, and beyond that the goods shed and its offices which are in different constructional styles to one another, and to the platform buildings. The platform, which has been extended in both directions at different times, is further evidence of the piecemeal way in which the station has evolved since 1869.

Above: We are looking from the box towards the platforms, with the GWR staff exchange apparatus in the foreground. When a train approaches, the engineman hangs out of the cab holding the staff with its loop carrier outermost. He slips the loop over the padded horn on the near post and lets go. The signalman later retrieves the token, puts it in his machine and blocks out, clearing the section. The lamp on the far post provides illumination at night. On the left is the double slip from the Up yard, and the goods shed, which is built of random stone. The buffer stops show that the goods shed has been taken

out of use, and the track truncated to serve as a headshunt and trap. Once again, this is a BoT rule, as every connection from goods sidings to a passenger line must be trapped to prevent a runaway coming into contact with a passenger train. Many modellers overlook these traps, as they take up space and seem to be a waste of money. Tucked between the goods shed and platform is the tightly curved spur into the carriage landing (points No 43). The signal between the down line and the bay line is the Up platform starter, and the bracket signal next to it is the splitting signal from the bay. The higher left hand arm reads to the main, and the

lower arm to the down sidings. The banner repeater disc is on the footbridge. The variation in the quality of the ballast between the main line and the sidings, and the fine screened gravel used in the cess, all merit attention, as this adds to the quality of a finished layout. Signal wires run from the box towards the station, and are another feature that is well worth modelling, though I must confess it is something I still have to attend to on our layout.

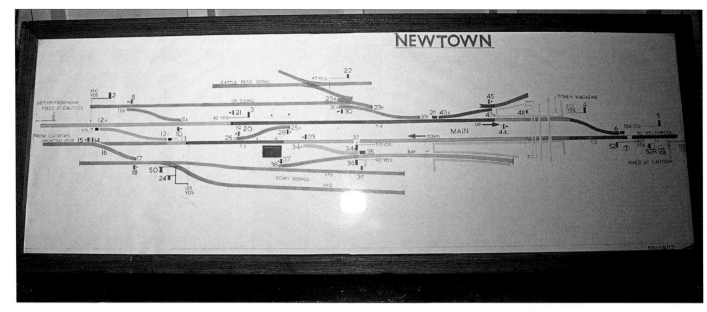

NEWTOWN

Above: Unlike Beverley, with its four level crossings, Newtown was not encumbered with level crossings. The signal box diagram locates various features. An approaching train at a passing station on a single track route usually had a straight run in, as it would be travelling faster than a departing train. In the early days, distants on single line routes were worked, but latterly, fixed distants were common, as the driver had to slow down to exchange the train staff, even if he was not stopping for traffic purposes. Signal No 4 is obscured by the footbridge, so a disc signal with a black bar, provides an advance warning of whether it is on or off. This is called a 'banner repeater', hence R4. The words 'Token Magazine' appear at the right hand end of the Down platform. If a train arrives from Caersws before a train arrives from Welshpool, the signalman cannot obtain a token for it until the westbound train has arrived. As soon as it has arrived he can offer the eastbound train to Welshpool, but if he withdrew a single line token from his instrument, he would have a long walk to hand it over, delaying the train. To reduce delays, an auxiliary token machine is placed in a hut at the end of the platform. When the signalman has obtained permission for the train to proceed, he instructs the driver to remove a token from the auxiliary instrument. I have emphasised the BoT hostility to facing points on passenger lines, but at Newtown there are two facing points as well as the loop points. At the west end of the loop, crossover 12 returns down trains to the main line. A shunting spur, reached off the end of a loop in this way is common. Facing points No 43, from the Up main to a horse and carriage landing by the Up platform, are unusual. In Victorian days, 25 crossover was near the station, and the dock was reached via a single slip from No 25. This would comply with BoT requirements. In later years, the obsession over facing points abated, and repositioning of the crossover explains why the facing point lock to 43 is lever No 26. Newtown is an exceptionally complex layout for a single line, but with the exception of the facing lead into the horse and carriage landing, points No 43, it follows the usual rules set out by the BoT. The modeller can adapt it for his layout, adding or subtracting features as space dictates.

Left: Newtown signal box was supplied by Dutton & Co, signal engineers of Worcester. It was a Dutton type 3 box, which was a design supplied to the Cambrian Railways between 1894 and 1901. Unlike many boxes on lines that were absorbed by the Great Western in 1923, and received standard GWR 'Reading' lever frames, Newtown retained its original Dutton frame. A view of the frame with its unusual curved-end catch handles appears on page 27 of the companion volume in this series *British Railway Signalling in Colour*. With the complex layout, it was a busy and important box, but sadly it succumbed to Radio Electronic Token Block working in 1988. The loss of traditional signalling and signal boxes always had a dramatic effect on the character of a station, as signalling equipment, more than any other aspect of railway infrastructure, helped to identify the parent company that had built a specific line.

Above: Although Dutton built Newtown box for the Cambrian Railways, the GWR resignalled the station. The bracket signal on the left has two arms. The left hand arm, No 39 is the smallest arm and this reflects its lesser importance. It is from the bay to the down sidings. The higher right hand arm, No 36, is from the bay platform to the main line via facing points No 34. To avoid confusion, it is lettered BAY. Although the finials and the signal fittings are standard Reading designs, the concrete post is rare for the GWR. During the First World War, shortages of timber and steel encouraged the railway companies to consider alternatives. William Marriott, chief engineer of the M&GN at Melton Constable works, had pioneered concrete signal posts with curing and weight reduction slots to this style before 1914, and it is known that M&GN concrete posts were supplied to the GCR, the GNR, the Midland, the SE&CR and Cambrian. This could be a Cambrian post that later received GWR fittings, but the GWR installed concrete posts itself in the early twenties, the most notable installation being at Aberystwyth. The posts were unpopular due to their great weight which complicated installation, whilst inadequate bushing means holes could go oval in use. With a wooden post, it was simple to drill and bush holes that wore. With a concrete post it was more complicated. The separate tubular post signal No 51, is the down main platform starter. To the right of No 51 is a ringed signal, No 22, the small arm and ring indicating that it is a siding signal. The Dutton type 3 signal box is visible in the distance, with a Wickham permanent way trolley standing alongside it.

Right: It was vital to know if the load on a wagon exceeded the loading gauge. If it did, goods might be knocked off if they come into contact with a bridge. Loading gauges might have posts of timber, concrete or second hand rail. On this rail built gauge, the post was drilled to take a horizontal length of gas piping about 15 feet above ground level. This was stayed to the top of the post by diagonal stay wires, and a metal framework was hung by wire or chain from the piping at the correct height. If the load on a wagon exceeded a safe height, it would strike the loading gauge, alerting the staff to the problem. Every goods depot would have a loading gauge in a strategic location. At Newtown, the gauge has a short length of ladder and a lamp half way up the post. This is of no use in illuminating the gauge by night, but is ideal to illuminate a staff catcher similar to the one we have seen on the down side. It is a rare instance of a loading gauge being put to a second purpose.

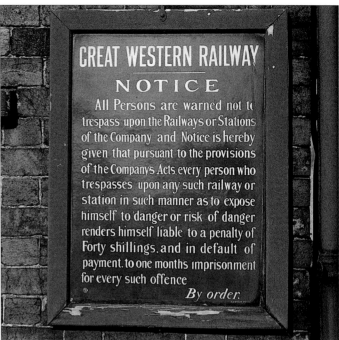

TAKE NOTICE

Above left: When I was a small boy, there always seemed to be a large cast iron notice at the end of the platform ramp telling me that I could be fined 40 shillings (£2) or cast into jail for one month. The 40 shillings would take a lot of pocket money, but seemed preferable to one month, but the penalties did seem disproportionate. As I got older, I realised that inflation from 1914 had played havoc with the value of money, and when most of these notices had been cast, 20 shillings, or £1 was a

weekly wage. Today, the hourly minimum legal wage in the United Kingdom is over four times as much, which gives us some idea of the collapse in the value of money over the past hundred years. Encouraged by a new Great Northern Railway Act, the officials at King's Cross decided that the unruly public should be warned in cast iron of the dire fate awaiting them if they misbehaved. In case someone got bored reading such an essay, a blunt BEWARE OF TRAINS plate was added. These classic signs were recorded at Bingham on 16th July 1974.

Above right: The Great Western Railway had style and manners, and whilst most stations displayed conventional cast iron notices, some places sported elegant enamelled notices, with white lettering on a dark blue ground. Rather than a blunt threat of punishment if you trespassed, the GWR politely explained that if someone trespassed in a way that exposed 'himself' to risk, he would be liable to fine or imprisonment. It may be that Paddington adopted the legal adage that 'the male included the female', or it may be that the idea that any lady would dream of trespassing upon the Great Western Railway was so preposterous that there was no need for such an exhortation. I have sometimes wondered why one station might receive cast iron notices, whilst another boasted the superior enamel version. Maybe the company had a supply of polite enamel notices for socially superior areas such as Chipping Campden in the Cotswolds, and a plainer version for areas of less social grace.

Left: As enthusiasts, we learn that British Railways came into being in 1948. In fact, the 1947 Transport Act set up the British Transport Commission, which operated through subsidiary Executives. These included the Railway Executive, the Road Transport Executive, the London Transport Executive, the Docks & Inland Waterways Executive, and the Hotels Executive. For most purposes, the Railway Executive used the title British Railways, and even painted it on the sides of their engines, until the lion and wheel insignia emerged. However, on solemn and sacred occasions, the awesome official wording appeared. The Railway Executive decided that it needed to warn people about trespassing, so it gave instructions to produce some cast iron notices. Whoever was told to cast the sacred notices, duly removed the discredited railway company title, and added 'The Railway Executive', but presumably no one had told him to read or amend the notice, which referred to the 'lines of railway of the Company'. Once again the penalty was 40 shillings, or one month. The separate speed limit sign would seem to serve little purpose, as the lettering is so small that it would hardly be visible to the enginemen.

Top right: At level crossings, or on public rights of way, pedestrians had a right to cross the line, so a threat of fine or imprisonment was out of order. However it was important that people should be aware of the danger posed by the trains, before venturing into the territory that they shared with the iron horse. Although the pre-grouping companies had produced thousands of such signs, the LNER felt the need for more, and this example went to Ulceby on the southern banks of the Humber. Once upon a time, cast iron signs were a trivial part of the railway scene, largely ignored by enthusiasts, railway men and passers' by. Today, most have gone, either for scrap, or into the hands of collectors, and it is only occasionally that we find a genuine pre-1948 or pre-group cast iron sign in use. Sadly, the few that do exist live on borrowed time, as they tend to vanish into the hands of the more unscrupulous collector, or are officially removed if they come to the attention of the powers-that-be. Colour schemes, and whether the original company name are picked out in white or left in body colour, seems to depend on the whim of the painter, or of the district officer concerned, and this adds a welcome note of diversity in a scene that is becoming ever more uniform.

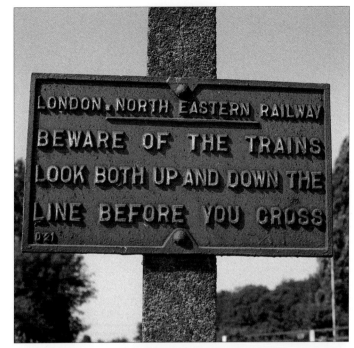

Centre right: The NER decided that the new fangled motor or other self propelled vehicle presented a dire threat to its warehouses at the Humber Dock in Hull, and warned the drivers that they must not enter the warehouse until told to do so by a servant of the company. Railway employees at this time were still commonly referred to as 'servants'. This was not a derogatory term, as we would understand now, but in the sense of one who serves, just as a soldier serves in the army. Why motor vehicles were such a menace that they needed a warning that horse drawn vehicles did not require, is unclear.

Bottom right: Instead of giving instruction, notices sometimes gave information. For ease of reference, and to avoid misunderstandings, bridges on each line were numbered consecutively. This GNR bridge plate survived at Rauceby in July 1989.

Bottom left: The BTC must have had a touching faith in the intellectual powers of their engines. As we read the wording of this notice, which is apparently directed to the engine itself, they must have reasoned that if there was a risk that an engine might stray on to badly maintained colliery tracks, the engine, rather than the driver, needed to be told what it could not do. This painted BTC notice was photographed at Moira on the MR line from Leicester to Burton in August 1973.

Bottom left and right: In March 1845, the Great North of Scotland Railway was formed to connect Aberdeen with Inverness. It was an Aberdonian venture, and unpopular in Inverness, where a route via Aviemore to the south was preferred. Parliament felt that the mountain route across the Cairngorms was premature, and the GNSR received its Act on 26th June 1846. The GNSR had big plans, but no money, so construction did not begin until 1852. By 1856, the GNSR had reached Keith, a distance of 53 miles, but was still 55 miles short of its target, and the difficult terrain lay ahead. Inverness had lost faith in the GNSR, and in 1854, the Inverness & Nairn received powers to build the first 15 miles out of Inverness, the line opening on 5th November 1855. The Inverness group proposed to continue to Elgin, covering half of the remaining gap, leaving the GNSR to build the rest. Given the later GNSR obsession to reach Elgin, it is ironic that the GNSR rejected this, so the Inverness & Aberdeen Junction Railway was authorised to build from Nairn to Keith on 21st July 1856. The line was completed on 18th August 1858. The GNSR had baulked at the cost of piercing the difficult terrain between Elgin and Keith, which included bridging the River Spey at Orton. They estimated that crossing the Spey would cost £160,000, and estimates were invariably exceeded. The I&AJ engineer, Joseph Mitchell, was an Inverness man who had worked with Thomas Telford on road building in the Highlands. He had an eye for the country, and chose a different route, which included a girder bridge with a 230 foot span, which was the longest single span yet built. His bridge also included six masonry arches of 30 feet for floodwaters, and cost £34,048, or one fifth of the GNSR estimate! Apart from completing the through route, the spread of 'Inverness' metals to Keith ensured that the GNSR would never reach Inverness, and that the country west and north of 'the capital of the Highlands', would be ruled by the Highland Railway, into which the I&AJ and other local companies were absorbed. The I&AJ was proud of the Spey viaduct, which was the last obstacle to through railway communication between London and Inverness, and placed ornamental plaques above the line at each end of the bridge. For an opening ceremony it was an ideal location, but they were invisible to the traveller unless he lay on the roof of the coach! In 1906, the Mitchell viaduct was replaced by a heavier structure, and both plaques were moved to Inverness. Given the Highland devotion to the kilt, one might expect the 'supporters', as they are called in heraldry, to wear Highland regalia, but the I&AJ 'supporters' wear a beard and a strategically placed laurel wreath, a costume which, however apt for the Garden of Eden, was not ideal for the Highlands. In Scottish heraldry, the arms of clan chieftains may have 'supporters', and in Scotland, the bearded man wearing a laurel wreath is a common 'supporter'. The arms represent powerful families in the district. The lion brandishing a sword, and motto Deus Juvavit (By God's assistance) belongs to the Clan MacDuff, as does the motto at the base of the device, Virtute et Opera (By virtue and by industry). The arm grasping a laurel wreath, and the motto Virtutis Regia Merces belong to Skene of Skene in Aberdeenshire, as do the three golden daggers with wolves' heads in the shield.

Top: So far, we have encountered Southern, North Eastern, Western, and LM Region notices in the appropriate regional house colours, so it is time we looked at the dark blue of the Eastern Region. This dark blue Eastern Region notice with the BRITISH RAILWAYS totem gave directions to Lincoln Central station.

Above: Sometimes, the railways desired a celebratory plaque to commemorate their deeds. This handsome plate in Southern Region green and white, was located near Southampton Town station, and was photographed on 22nd July 1972. It commemorated the opening of a bridge to the public by agreement with Southampton Corporation, and the great, the good and those who did the work, were duly honoured.

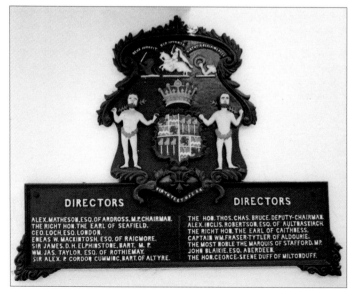

A LARGE CITY TERMINAL

In presenting some medium sized stations, I realised that several views were necessary to show the station adequately, and at a big city terminal, it is more complex. Rather than cover several stations inadequately, I have explored a single city terminus. Obviously, the exact details of the frontage, station hotel, cab rank, main concourse, booking offices, platforms and approach tracks differ from station to station, but in gaining a clear insight into one station, we are better equipped to understand others. The station I have chosen is Glasgow Central. It is a remarkable example of outstanding design on a limited site.

Right: One of the benefits of being a doctor's son, was that I was sometimes taken to meet interesting patients. I once met a pensioner who showed us his campaign medals from the Sudan and the Boer War. On many occasions I visited a model railway in a garden shed. Its creator, Arthur Forsythe, had been brought up alongside the Caledonian Railway. He had seen *Cardean*, and the legendary No 123, and instilled into me the pride that Caley men felt in their stylish and powerful railway. Indeed I was never quite sure if the Caledonian had adopted Scottish blue, or if Scotland had adopted Caledonian blue. Arthur's first love was the Calendar & Oban railway, but Glasgow Central, was another favourite. Arthur spoke of wooden panelling, and of the 'Hielanman's umbrella'. In its imperious march into central Glasgow, the Caledonian was carried over Argyle Street, that great thoroughfare that runs from east to west through the city. No fewer than 13 tracks, with their associated platforms, a cab rank and a magnificent train shed, were carried above the road on a massive bridge. So long was the bridge that when the skies opened, the canny Highlander would make for Argyle Street, and while his time away beneath Central station. On this sunny day, there was no fear of rain, but looking from the west towards the 'Hielanman's umbrella', I could recall Arthur's words vividly. In his day, there was the added bonus of a fleet of over 1,000 tramcars, and Argyle Street was one of the principal routes.

Below right: Arthur Forsythe could list the names of the great thoroughfares that bounded Central station. To the east was Union Street, which recalled the union of England and Scotland in 1707. Beyond that was Jamaica Street, a reminder of Glasgow's status as a great sea port. To the west was Hope Street, and the Caledonian's mighty Central Station Hotel rearing up almost seven stories. At one time, it had almost 400 rooms, and its roofline stood 116 feet above street level. It was five years in building, opening on 19th June 1885, and its tower at the north end of the site, on the corner of Hope and Gordon Streets was 129 feet high. It was electrically lit from new, and even boasted an elevator. Fire precautions that would be rare fifty years later were routine. The corridors on the upper floors were of concrete slabs laid on iron joists, and when the station was enlarged between 1901 and 1907, the hotel was extended and received more fireproofing. The original architect was Sir Rowand Anderson, one of Scotland's leading architects, and the turn-of-the-century extensions were the work of James Miller. We are looking north from Argyle Street along Hope Street. The modern fire escape, though an important addition to the hotel's safety features, is unsightly, and it is a pity it did not match this magnificent hotel, which is a listed Grade B structure. The paired round headed windows of the train shed wall are as stylish as the hotel. The tall arch near the BR double arrow is the entrance to the cab rank, added during the 1901-1906 rebuilding.

Above: The main entrance to Glasgow Central is on Gordon Street, a cast iron porte cochere projecting over a short reception road. At the date of this view, 21st May 1977, the area around central station retained its Victorian and Edwardian elegance, and the BRITISH RAILWAYS CENTRAL STATION lettering, which was installed soon after nationalisation, projected proudly above the awning. The main entrance to Central Station Hotel was just feet away on the corner of Gordon Street and Hope Street. The Caledonian had appropriated the Lion Rampant of Scotland to its own use, and this powerful piece of heraldry, set in a gilt wreath, proclaimed the pride, the power and the glory of the Caledonian Railway. The warm red sandstone, of which so many of Glasgow's buildings are made, adds to the sheer pleasure of studying these magnificent buildings.

Below left: Standing on to the concourse, Arthur Forsythe's descriptions of polished wood panelling curving away in all directions came alive. We are looking from the concourse towards the panelled booking office, which at one time made the proud boast 'Tickets to ALL stations in Scotland'. An arrow which is just out of view, and the prominent CENTRAL HOTEL inscription above the first floor windows, points passengers to the entrance to the hotel from the concourse. To the right of the booking office are two arches of the entrance from Gordon Street. A further arch exists on the far side of the booking office. Until the 1870s, the Caley approach to the city centre had been poor. Construction of a rail bridge carrying the Caley to the north bank of the Clyde began in 1876, and the original Central station opened in December 1879. Despite an impressive frontage on to Gordon St and the equally imposing Central Hotel, the station, which was provided with 8 short platforms, and a cramped concourse, was inadequate for the traffic it handled. In 1889, a ninth platform was squeezed in, but salvation came between 1901 and 1906. Under the inspired direction of Donald A Matheson, the Caledonian engineer-in-chief, the station was enlarged to the south and west. An extra four platforms were added, as was a second bridge over the Clyde. Impressive though all this was, Matheson's enlargement included two strokes of genius. At most large terminals, the platforms end in line, and passenger flows cross one another, creating congestion. Matheson realigned the tracks so that the platforms ended in echelon. He was a shrewd observer of human behaviour, explaining 'the tendency of people to spread like flowing water and travel along the line of least resistance was kept in view. It was therefore thought desirable to have curved building lines and rounded corners not only in the concourse, but also in the subway and elsewhere in the station'. The booking office with its rounded corners is evidence of Matheson's genius.

Above: Arthur Forsythe had told me of a panelled destination indicator. Over fifty years after the demise of the Caledonian Railway, it was still in use when I photographed it on 21st May 1977. Its 74 ft length contained a special announcements section, a short display for arriving trains, and thirteen windows for departing trains, each with its platform number displayed below it. Departure times were given at the top, whilst destinations were displayed on linen blinds that were inserted into the frames behind the glass by hand. It must have been labour intensive and hard work to operate, but it was magnificent and a delight to read. As I studied it, I began to understand Arthur's comments about an elongated pear drop.

Bottom right: To the left of the entrance from Gordon Street was another polished wood arcade. This housed the left luggage office and other station facilities. It was a worthy match for the booking office and destination screen, and added balance to this side of the station. Without it, the concourse would have seemed unfinished. The absence of columns supporting the train shed roof, which was possible because of the massive lattice girders that spanned the entire width of the site, removed a common obstacle to free flow within the concourse of a large station, and created a light and airy effect.

Inset right: For generations, travellers passing through London have met 'under the clock at Waterloo'. For Glaswegians, the meeting place was 'the Shell'. This was a First World War 15in Beardmore artillery shell that had been converted to a collecting box for the Ladies Auxiliary Association to provide help for sick

children. So legendary was it that the mere words 'THE Shell' sufficed. Glasgow lost its beloved tramcars in 1962, and when BR moved 'the shell' from its central position in the concourse to a side location near the left luggage office where we see it in 1974, there was an outcry. Some years later 'the shell' was reinstated in its proper place. The modeller producing a large station could add such a feature with great effect.

Above: Apart from remodelling the concourse in 1901-1906, Donald Matheson added four new platforms, Nos 10-13. Two rows of octagonal steel columns separated the old station from the new, the rows being on the left hand side in this view. Platforms 10 and 11 are just to the right of the columns. By 1977, the cab rank, which was between platforms 11 and 12, had become a car park, the sloping entrance from Hope Street being on the extreme right of the view. Although straight lattice girders had been used on the high roof above the concourse, the girders were much lower over the platforms, and Matheson created a light and graceful effect by using an elliptical curve, whilst the glazed screen between the columns was decorated with a radial pattern.

Below: We are looking from platform 10 towards the cab rank and the buffer stops in July 1995. The graceful nature of the elliptical roof girders is apparent now that they no longer collect the grime from steam locomotives. Although Central station is widely regarded as Matheson's most outstanding work, he was a talented engineer with a fine record. He was born at Perth in 1860 and attended Heriot Watt College in Edinburgh before joining the LNWR for a brief period. Returning to Scotland, he became Engineer-in-Chief of the CR in 1899, and in 1910 made the unusual transition from Chief Engineer to General Manager. With the formation of the LMS, he became General Manager Scotland, retiring in 1926.

Above: Looking from platform 9, we see the old station with paired platforms 8/7, 6/5, 4/3 and 2/1. The long faces, which are used for the principal express trains are 1, 2, and 9-11, which are between 913 and 1160 feet in length, platforms 3-8 being from 405 to 610 feet in length. Describing Glasgow Central station has brought back many happy memories to me of listening to Arthur Forsythe, a charming and skilled Scottish modeller, who knew and loved the Caley in its heyday. When I listened to Arthur speak of the 'Hielanman's Umbrella', the woodwork at Central or of his beloved Callander & Oban, it never occurred to me that I would have the chance to share his thoughts with a wider audience. This coverage of Glasgow Central is dedicated to the memory of a delightful Scottish modeller. Happily, one of the engines he built runs on our model railway to this day.

Right: We are looking from platforms 9/10 south across the Clyde bridge. The original railway bridge of 1878 was built of wrought iron lattice girders resting on cast iron pillars, and carried four tracks. During the 1901-06 rebuilding, a new eight-track bridge was added parallel to, and just west of the original structure. By the late 1950s, the original bridge was in poor condition. In 1961, a new colour light signalling system and a new box came into use, the enhanced line capacity they provided making it possible to abandon the 1878 bridge. So flexible was Matheson's echeloned layout, that little work was needed

to realign the tracks from platform 1 and 2 on to the later bridge the lattice girders of which are visible on the left. Work on a new power box to replace almost 100 existing boxes, including Glasgow Central began in 1970 as a part of the upgrading process prior to the introduction of 25kv electric services. One of the fascinating aspects of railway infrastructure is that whilst the locomotives, carriages and

wagons of pre-grouping and pre-nationalisation days have long since been taken out of traffic, the infrastructure that the Victorian and Edwardian engineers provided is still in daily use. After a long period when so-called experts derided Victorian style as heavy and fussy, we now have a better appreciation of the quality of their work, and of its lasting qualities.

PERMANENT WAY

The term 'permanent way' came into use to make a distinction between the contractor's trackwork laid down during the construction of a railway, and the 'permanent' track installed prior to the line being handed over for use. In reality, whilst some components could last for decades, and I have known of 100 year old rails in sidings, and of pre-group rail chairs, trackwork is anything but permanent.

Rails are worn away by heavy traffic, or the webs of rails can rust until the rail collapses. Metal fatigue can lead to rail breakages. Wooden sleepers can rot. Steel sleepers, although rare in the British Isles until recent years, can corrode. Concrete sleepers, if they are not well supported by ballast, can fracture. As with every other aspect of railway infrastructure, it is an immense topic, and has been the subject of many works for the professional engineer, though little has been written for the enthusiast.

The earliest 'track' consisted of wooden battens laid on transverse planks, and had come into use by the 1630s. By the 1730s, thin pieces of iron were being nailed to battens to increase their life, and the first cast iron rails were cast at Coalbrookdale in 1767. Because of the limitation of iron working, the rails were two to three feet in length, the joints being supported on wooden sleepers. The edge rail came a few years later. This was an 'L' section rail, the wheels being devoid of flanges. A wagon with such wheels could run on road or rail, but mud and small stones built up in the angle of the 'L'. From about 1800 the use of stone blocks instead of wooden sleepers became common. Although these primitive systems offered an advance on rough unmade roads, they were weak and unsuited to heavy or fast traffic.

By the time the railway age dawned, iron founding had made great strides, and it was no longer necessary to cast rails in short lengths. This, as much as the steam locomotive, made railways feasible. Three types of rail evolved within a few years of one another. One was to carry the fastest trains in the world for a time, but was to fade into obscurity. The second became the standard British rail for over a century. The third was frowned upon as inferior in its native land for a century, but was to spread across the globe, and then triumph in Britain.

Top left: Since time immemorial, primitive man smelted iron by using charcoal. To produce limited quantities of iron by this costly method, vast swathes of land had been deforested. It was only in the 18th century after successive generations of the Darby family of Coalbrookdale had perfected the smelting of iron using coal and coke, that iron became economical to produce, and the fuel problem was overcome. Even so, the furnaces produced tiny quantities of iron. The best that the technology of the day could offer was rails that were perhaps three feet long. They were carried in metal chairs resting on stone blocks. To provide strength, given the crude casting techniques, the bottom surface of the rail bowed down in the centre 'in a fish belly' shape, from which early rails took their name. As iron founding improved, it was possible to cast longer rails, but the fishbelly shape was retained, the rail being supported on cast iron chairs between each 'belly'. This type of rail was used at the dawn of the steam age, but soon fell out of favour. One place where it survived was on the Stratford & Morteon Railway. This horse worked line was authorised in 1821, and opened in 1826. It was taken over by the Oxford, Worcester & Wolverhampton Railway in 1846, and once the OW&W line from Stratford to Honeybourne was completed in 1859, the northern section was superfluous. Surprisingly, it survived as a horse worked anachronism, and although little used after 1904, the tracks remained in situ until the First World War. One of the tramway wagons was preserved on a length of track at Stratford-on-Avon.

Above left: Isambard Kingdom Brunel was an unusual combination of visionary and practical man. He was a superb engineer who had known triumph and failure in the dank Wapping tunnel that his father was driving under the River Thames, and a relative latecomer to railways. When Stephenson was already celebrated as a railway engineer, Brunel was virtually unknown, yet it was Brunel who envisaged high-speed intercity expresses whilst his contemporaries thought of coal trains. Paradoxically, the coal they saw as the lifeblood of railways is as much a thing of the past, as is the Brunelian idea for high speed trains. Brunel rejected the 4 foot 8½ inch standard gauge adopted by the Stephensons and other engineers, and developed the 7 foot 0¼ inch broad gauge. To achieve stability for his road bed, Brunel abandoned stone blocks or transverse wooden sleepers in favour of rails laid on longitudinal timber baulks, the track being kept in gauge by transverse ties, or transoms. The baulks, which were 14 in x 7 in in cross section, were 30 foot in length, and provided continuous support for the rail, rather than merely at every transverse sleeper. With continuous support, Brunel could use a flat rail with a wide foot, which could be much lighter per foot than the heavy rail supported at intervals in conventional track. When his contemporaries were using rails of 80 lb per foot, Brunel was laying rail of 45 to 68 lb per foot, and operating the fastest trains in the world. The rail was shaped like an inverted U with prominent flanges at each side. It was called Bridge Rail and was virtually indestructible. Long after the broad gauge was a memory, and bridge rail had been taken out of track use, thousands of lengths remained in use as fence posts, or to support cast iron notices. Two sections of bridge rail had been bolted back to back to form this fence post, which was photographed at Appleford on 27th July 1989, a century after the last length of bridge rail had been rolled.

Bottom: The discovery of some broad gauge track that had been buried and forgotten permitted the Great Western Society to recreate a section of Brunel's permanent way at the Didcot railway centre. In the previous view we saw the 'top hat' shape of bridge rail, and how the flanges were drilled at intervals. The rail was bolted to the baulk, producing a rigid road that should have been suited for high speed running. However, Brunel made a serious mistake. To anchor the track, he drove vertical piles into the formation. They were intended to hold the track down and prevent sideways movement. Because a weak gravel ballast was used, and packing was inadequate by modern standards, the ballast settled beneath the longitudinals. This left them supported by the piles, which were located in the seven foot space between the rails. Instead of a rigid roadbed, Brunel had created a flimsy timber viaduct that gave a dreadful ride, and within four years, the piles were cut away from the track. Thereafter, the baulk road gave a good ride, as Brunel had envisaged. Financial interests, and the desire to carve out territory for different companies, caused rivalry between competing companies, but the hostility was especially fierce where the broad gauge was involved. Brunel was a flamboyant showman, and his advocacy of the superiority of his broad gauge over the 'narrow gauge' as the Stephenson gauge was contemptuously referred to, antagonised the railway community. The red painted chock pivoted on the left hand side of the rail, which is swung through 90 degrees by the crank and point rodding was an early alternative to the catch point. Bridge rail is sometimes confused with Barlow rail, after William Henry Barlow (1812-1902) who patented a saddle backed version with a sweeping curve in 1849. It was little used on the GWR.

Above: Brunel's opponents claimed that the standard gauge was well established, and that if a second broader gauge developed, freight and passengers would need to be transhipped wherever a break of gauge existed. A Royal Commission examined this problem. They were impressed by the speed of the broad gauge trains, and the way this had led to improved performance on the narrow gauge, adding that the public were indebted to 'the genius of Mr Brunel', but a black propaganda campaign from the narrow gauge faction, which included carefully staged chaos at a tranship point, led the 'Gauge Commission' to describe break of gauge as a serious evil. Permission was given for extensions in existing broad gauge areas, but not elsewhere. In the border territories, many routes had to be built as mixed gauge. This did not simply mean laying an additional rail. It produced complex track formations, as this track at Didcot reveals. Instead of the single frog of a normal point, four Frogs, or Vees, are required, adding to construction and maintenance costs. During Brunel's lifetime, the GWR remained true to the broad gauge, but Daniel Gooch, the GWR's legendary locomotive engineer and later chairman, raised the idea of gauge conversion at a general meeting in 1866. Conversion started in 1868, but it was not until Friday 20th May 1892, that the last broad gauge train ran.

Although the broad gauge had stagnated after Brunel's death, the lead over its rivals meant it was still competitive, and many Great Western men were truly distressed to see their birthright pass into oblivion.

Opposite page top: Standard gauge devotees took a different approach. Early fish bellied rail had been supported in cast iron chairs at intervals of under three feet. As technology advanced, the fish bellied concept was dropped, but the idea of supporting rail in cast iron chairs was firmly established. Double-headed rail, with a bulbous head and an identical base, the two being joined by a thinner web, was tried. When the head was worn down by traffic, the rail could be turned upside down, the unworn base becoming the new head, adding years of further life. This seemed foolproof, but like Brunel's piles, had a fatal flaw. The impact of countless wheels on the rail slapped the base of the rail firmly on to the chairs every time a wheel passed over a length of track. This pumping motion indented the base of the rail, and when it was turned, it gave an uncomfortable and noisy ride. Engineers rejected double headed rail, preferring a rail where the head received more metal at the expense of the foot. Although it could not be inverted, the greater wearing surface of the bigger head outlasted a

doubleheaded rail, that could be turned. The rail with the bigger head was called 'bullhead' rail and would fit existing rail chairs. This portrait of the junction at Canning Street North box, in the Birkenhead Docks shows bullhead rail trackwork. The wing rail of the 'Vee' in the foreground shows the cross section of bullhead rail. The greater amount of metal in the head as compared to the foot is obvious. The rail sits in a cast iron chair, and is held in place by a 'key'. Originally keys were wooden, but latterly a coiled steel key has been used. Most keys in this scene are wooden, but at the 'Vee', the key is metal. Although some companies used inside keyed track, where the keys were in the 'four foot', as the space between the rails is called, most companies preferred outside keyed track, with the keys on the outer side of the rail. Some rails appear to be 'inside keyed' at this junction, but they are checkrails, and the running rails are outside keyed as usual.

Opposite page bottom: Traffic growth led to ever more complex formations, as at Overseal on the MR Ashby & Nuneaton line. The station, photographed on 26th August 1973, served the Leicestershire coal field, and from right to left, the formation includes a double slip, a three way point, a single slip and another double slip, the latter providing access to a short headshunt with a rail-built bufferstop.

Above: The earliest railways served industry, and passenger traffic was an afterthought, but high speed running, well laid tracks and complex junctions meant that public railways soon departed from their roots. To savour railways as they had been at the dawn of the railway age, it was necessary to explore industrial systems, and particularly narrow gauge lines. The Leighton Buzzard Narrow Gauge Railway is a well known preserved line today, but started life in 1919 as a joint venture between two sand companies, Joseph Arnold & Sons Ltd and George Garside (Sand) Ltd to convey sand from their many quarries to the LNWR at Billington Road. Arnold No 16, Motor Rail (Simplex) No 4709 of 1936 is moving loaded skip wagons at Arnold's Double Arches quarry on 29th September 1973. The uneven track, which is partially buried in sand, is typical of industrial systems, and much better than many comparable lines I have encountered over the years.

Below: In 1968, Arnold's permitted enthusiasts to operate weekend passenger services. Public services never ran south of Page's Park, but until the Billington Road section was lifted, a few engineering trains, such as this working seen passing Pratt's Pit near Billington Road on 31st May 1970, were operated. Until 1967, there had been three tracks to the right of the engine, but two had been abandoned that year, and the old main line had been declared unsafe in 1968, due to the subsiding quarry face just to the right of the engine.

Top: 'A chair is a chair is a chair!' Far from it! The humble rail chair shows great diversity. The function of a chair in bullhead track is to spread the axleload over a sufficient surface area of the sleeper by means of a wide cast iron base, and in conjunction with the key, to keep the rail to gauge. The upper surface of the base is slightly concave. This should match the bottom of the rail, so that the rail is supported over the whole base, and is canted inwards at an angle of 1 in 20 to 1 in 24. Railway tyres are slightly coned so that the wheels are self centring, and the canting of the rail is to assist in this process. Early chairs weighed 14 - 18 lb, or a third to a half of the weight of the rail in use per yard length. To give an example, the Leicester & Swannington Railway used 35lb/yard rail and 14lb chairs in 1832. In 1840, the Birmingham & Gloucester was laid using 17lb chairs and 56lb rail. As speeds and axle loads grew, rail weights increased, and the Midland 'Bedford & London' extension used 83lb rail and a 34lb chair in 1868. Early chairs were secured to the sleepers by one spike or bolt on each side of the rail. Two hole chairs of this sort have long been obsolete. This is one of the few surviving Isle of Wight Railway Co chairs of this type. It is a held down by two chair screws, one on each side of the rail.

Centre: By 1875, the two hole chair was inadequate for main line use, and companies such as the Midland and the LNWR switched to four hole chairs. The Settle & Carlisle railway, which was built less than a decade after the Midland London extension, was laid in 40lb four-hole chairs. Although the jaw remained the same size, the base area of the chair that rested on the sleeper was significantly enlarged, reducing the risk of the chair cutting into the sleeper under heavy loading. By the 1890s, some companies were laying 100lb rail carried in 54lb four-hole chairs. This LNWR chair, which was cast in 1902, and was photographed at Bicester on 3rd August 1970, is held in place by two chair screws and two round headed track spikes. Although the jaw is the same width as a two hole chair, the foot of the four hole chair widens out to provide sufficient metal for two holes on each side.

Below: The bigger foot of the four hole chair was better than the two hole chair, but many engineers felt that two additional spikes were not ideal. Between 1905 and 1922, various British Standards were drawn up for track components, including the British Standard three hole chair. Instead of the two screws and two spikes, it was secured to the sleeper by three chair screws. The three hole chair shared the enlarged foot of the four hole version, but reduced the risk of splitting the sleeper by not having two pairs of holes in line within a few inches. I photographed this British Standard LSWR chair at Dorchester in May 1975. It is secured to the track by three chair screws and has a plain un-ribbed inner jaw. It is lettered L. S. W. R., with stops appearing after each letter. The rail is held in place by a wooden key that has seen better days. When it is only possible to see the inside face of a 3 or 4 hole chair, it is hard to distinguish them, but a 3 hole chair will be held by bolts, whilst a 4 hole chair will be held by a square or hexagonal headed bolt and a round headed spike. The GWR used a two hole chair with a wide base. This had a serrated base that fitted into serrations on the upper face of the sleeper, and instead of a chair screw, it was secured by two through bolts. As was so often the case, the GWR did it their way, and it was usually a better way. A GWR 2 hole chairs appear in the view of Westbury shed on page 11.

Left: Given the need for selection, it may seem excessive to allocate two views to LSWR chairs, but this is another BS standard with three chair screws. Unlike the previous chair, it has a ribbed inner jaw, whilst the bulge on the key jaw is more bulbous. It is lettered L&SWR, with no stops, but with the ampersand. This time a spring metal key is used to hold the rail in place. It was photographed at Sandown in the Isle of Wight in 1994. Wooden sleepers were traditionally of Baltic pine (pinus sylvestris), Jarrah, Scotch Fir or Larch. The term Scotch is normally only applied to whisky, 'Scottish' being preferred in other instances, but Scotch Fir was the accepted term used by railwaymen. Jarrah is an Australian wood with exceptional lasting properties, whilst home produced Larch was cheaper but not so long-lasting. In theory, a sleeper should be twice the rail gauge, so the ideal length for a standard gauge sleeper would be 9ft 5in. Until the First World War, the standard dimensions were 9ft x 10in x 5in. Due to supply shortages in 1914-18, the railway companies accepted 8ft 6in sleepers, and this became the standard from 1921. The 'rivet counter' who loves to criticise other modellers may wish to check if he has the correct 2, 3 or 4 hole chairs, and whether his sleepers are correct or up to six inches out, lest his victim do so for him!

Centre: With bullhead track, rail joints can be suspended, semi-supported or supported. In a suspended joint, the ends of the rails are carried by chairs each side of the fishplate. The chairs are standard, and this has been standard on bullhead track for many years. In the semi-supported joint, which was common in pre-grouping days, (and was sometimes used by BR on early jointed flat bottomed track), the sleepers were closer to the rail ends, and the chairs were cast with wider jaws to hold the ends of the fishplates as well as the rails. With the supported joint, the sleeper was directly below the joint, and a special rail joint chair was required. At the dawn of the railway age, when fishbellied rail was produced in single spans, every chair was a joint chair, but when it became possible to roll longer rails, a distinction grew up between joint chairs, which supported a rail joint, and ordinary rail chairs. Joint chairs were wider and 25 to 50% heavier than standard chairs. Supported joints have long been obsolete, and are seldom found even in sidings, so this South Eastern & Chatham Railway three hole supported joint chair is a remarkable survivor. BoT rules required that rails should be joined by fishplates. Here, the rails are joined by four-bolt fishplates, the outer bolts being normal round-headed bolts. This may seem strange, but there is a lug on the shaft of the bolt which engages in an oval hole in the fishplate, which prevents it turning as the nut is tightened up. The two inner bolts are square headed and extra long, as they pass through both fishplates, the rail and through the joint chair. The misalignment of the rails shows that whatever its theoretical benefits, the joint chair is no substitute for proper alignment and maintenance.

Below: The civil engineer does not like points, as they are costly to build and require special components. The standard S1 chair for 95lb bullhead rail is 14½in long and 8in wide and weighs 46lb, and is ideal for most track conditions. The L1 bridge chair was developed for use where the maximum width of the chair seating is limited, for example on a bridge with longitudinal timbering. The L1 is 10½in long, but is 11in wide, as it is secured by four bolts to the timbering. Although called bridge chairs, the main use of the L1 is in pointwork where rails are converging, and there is not enough room for two conventional S1 chairs. An even more compact chair, the M1, was produced, its dimensions being 10 x 8¾in. Because of the limited bearing surface, the M1 can cut into the sleeper, so is rarely used. Special check rail chairs are also required, as the gap between the running rail and check rail is just 1¾in. Check rail chairs are given a C coding. This view, at Northampton on 1st May 1976, demonstrates the use of these different types of chair. Without a tape measure, it is difficult to distinguish an L1 from an M1 in a perspective view, but my impression is that these are the L1 chairs, with C type check rail chairs closer to the frogs or 'V' blocks. As we look at this point, we can understand why the civil engineer prefers plain track, or if he must have points, that they should be normal points. Sadly there are many places where space demands single or double slips, three way points or other abominations. As any modeller knows, they save space, and whilst we have problems when designing our layouts, our 12 inch to the foot cousins have similar worries.

Top: Charles Blacker Vignoles was born in Co Wexford, Ireland in 1793, and had wide engineering experience in the United States, Europe and South America, as well as the UK. He questioned whether double headed or bullhead rail was ideal, and in 1837, patented a flat bottom rail (FB). Vignoles dispensed with chairs, by providing a wide flat base for the rail. Vignoles rails were adopted throughout Europe, whilst the American engineer R L Stevens, popularised a similar design in the States. In England, Vignoles rails received little support. Prejudice and practicality both played a part. England had been at war with France from 1793 to 1815, and Vignoles' French sounding name and extensive engineering practice in Europe can have been no help, nor did the claim that FB rail could be spiked directly to sleepers, rather than mounted in a carefully positioned and screwed chair. The UK railways had a commanding lead over foreign lines for speed and quality, and there was a feeling that whilst flat bottom rails spiked to a sleeper that might be a rough hewn log, was good enough for foreigners, it was not acceptable here. Although Vignoles rails were rejected by the big companies, they appealed to impecunious standard gauge lines and many narrow gauge concerns. Once such company was the Isle of Man Railway. Shortage of funds had forced the IOMR to give up one of its three intended routes (to Ramsey), the remaining two lines opening in 1873 and 1874. Vignoles flat bottom rail was specified. In most places, rail was spiked direct to half round wooden sleepers, saving in construction costs, but where conditions required it, such as on the 86 foot lattice girder bridge over the River Dhoo near Quarter Bridge on the Peel line, the IOMR showed there was no problem in marrying flat bottom rail and chairs. The line closed in 1968, the viaduct being demolished in 1974-75.

Centre: The Cotswolds are Great Western territory, but located near the peaceful Gloucestershire village of Aston Magna was another user of Vignoles flat bottom rail. The Gloucestershire Brick & Tile Co was not on the same par as the great brickworks in the vicinity of Bedford, but remained in production into the early 1970s. It operated a two foot gauge industrial railway connecting the brick works with the quarry. Motor Rail 'Simplex' 8724 of 1941, which was variously named *Flower Power* or *Thunderbird 5*, and was the sole remaining engine in working order, is seen at the plant on 1st August 1970. The flat bottomed two foot gauge track is spiked directly to wooden sleepers.

Below: One has to admit that the permanent way of the Gloucestershire Brick & Tile Co main line left a little to be desired, and derailments may not have been unknown, but having looked at a variety of other main lines, it makes an interesting comparison. The route ran from the plant to the quarry, the location of which is marked by the jib of the excavator visible in the distance. I cannot help but smile as I look at these two views. In this volume, we have looked at railways built over bogs and in deep cuttings. We have seen the sweeping curves of the Settle & Carlisle Railway, and complex pointwork in Northampton. In each case the trackwork is a joy to behold. As we look at the Aston Magna railway, the question must be, 'how did it stay on the track'. It is closely followed by a second question, 'is it possible to model track like this and expect anything to remain on it'. If, you, as a modeller are inspired to create something like this, do please tell me.

Top: From the 1880s, railway engineers studied progress overseas, regularly visiting US and European railways. In the 1920s, GWR officers advocated laying American flat bottom track to obtain comparative data under British conditions, and experimental lengths later appeared. The results encouraged BR to adopt FB rail as standard in 1948. Rail joints have always been a nuisance, as fracture lines radiate from the fishplate bolt holes, so welded rail joints also became BR policy. Welding reduces the number of joints, and offers a smoother ride, and modern practice is to weld several lengths of flat bottom rail, or to lay long stretches of continuously welded rail. Steel expands as the temperature rises, and with traditional fishplated track, a small gap is left at the rail joints to allow for expansion in hot weather. Without the gap, the rail would still expand, but being restricted by adjacent rails, which are also trying to expand, the expansion forces will become so great that the rail will burst its fastenings and deform. On very hot days when expansion exceeds the gap, this can happen. Although a simple expansion gap is adequate for rails of 40 to 60 feet, welded rail presents problems for whilst it is pre-stressed when laid to minimise expansion problems, a gap is still necessary, but this cannot take the form of a simple joint with a gap in it. Where welded rails exceed 183 metres, a lapped joint, called an adjustment switch, is provided at the ends of each welded length, and at intervals of not more than 730m in the welded section. This adjustment switch was photographed at Lowdham on 3rd July 1989. Unlike light railways, modern FB rail for heavy duty lines is mounted on bedplates to provide an adequate shoulder to spread the axle load. The rails are held in place by Pandrol clips, which became the BR standard for concrete and wood sleepers in 1964/65. At the joints, the rails are tapered and overlapped to support the wheel. As the metal expands, the rails slide towards one another in the fabricated joint chairs. The wires connecting the rails are track circuit bonds, the swan neck curve taking up expansion and contraction stresses. Although the line has been laid using concrete sleepers, the adjustment switch uses creosoted wooden sleepers which are held together by a couple of short length of bullhead rail, providing a welcome contrast between the two rail types.

Centre: The Isle of Man Railway had combined FB rail and chairs to provide a rigid road on the Dhoo river bridge on the outskirts of Douglas. Away from the narrow gauge, where strange things can occur, many enthusiasts would say that chairs and flat bottom rail are mutually incompatible. Whilst such a combination was rare on British Rail, as the design of FB rail is to permit it to be secured directly to the sleeper or to rest on a flat bedplate, it is technically possible, as this view demonstrates. It is however very rare, and even the 500 plus page manual of the Permanent Way Institution does not refer to it. The chair is an LNER three-hole design manufactured in 1935. The FB rail is secured in place by two coiled steel keys that are hammered in from opposite ends of the chair, but with the coil vertical rather than horizontal. This illustration was taken on the former GN line at Bottesford on 4th July 1989.

Below: If a signalman said he had 'shot the train', he was not acting like a Wild West gunslinger, but explaining that he had placed a detonator on the track to give the driver an emergency warning to stop. Detonators are a giant version of the percussion cap used in a child's six-shooter, and are secured to the rail by lead straps. When the locomotive runs over the detonator, it explodes the charge, the loud bang attracting the driver's attention. On a multi-track line, if a signalman needed to shoot a train on a distant track, he could not be expected to risk life or limb crossing in front of other trains, or in trying to fix the detonator as the train bore down on him. A detonator placer was a mechanical device that was actuated by a detonator placer lever in the signal box. We have illustrated a detonator placer lever at Beverley. Here is a detonator placer machine with the top cover removed. The operating rod in the foreground is connected to the placer, and when the signalman pulls his lever, the detonators are pulled forward and above the rail. When the engine arrives, the wheel strikes the detonator, and bang! The detonator placer is a 'one use' machine and has to be reloaded after each firing, but in the nature of much emergency equipment, is seldom used, so this is not a serious problem. Strangely enough modern practice is to dispense with them.

TEMPLES OF STEAM

Like pagan temples, the shrines to the new Gods of nineteenth century inventiveness sprang up from Penzance to Thurso, and from the West of Ireland to East Anglia. The steam locomotive gained a hold on popular imagination that it has never lost. Generations of small boys grew up desiring to be high priests of the faith, taking the iron horse on its perambulations. Others grew up longing to model it or photograph it. Almost forty years have passed since the last standard gauge steam engine turned a wheel in commercial service on British Railways, yet the attraction still remains, and steam railtours attract thousands of people to the lineside. Whatever the magic, steam lives on, and most modellers want a motive power depot on their layout. As many modellers do not appreciate the layout principles of a shed, or what work has to be done, I have followed the movements of an engine as it comes on shed.

Above: Motive power depots varied from gigantic sheds such as Liverpool Edge Hill, or Crewe South, which housed hundreds of engines, to branch sub-sheds with one locomotive. The original LSWR shed at Bournemouth opened with Bournemouth Central station in 1885, and was on a cramped site on the north side of the main line to Weymouth. Between 1936 and 1938, it was rebuilt by the Southern Railway. The shed, which is depicted on 28th October 1966, was a four road brick building that was re-roofed by BR in asbestos panels on a steel framework. To the right of the shed, the top of the 1938 water softening tower peeps up above the lifting road, whilst a variety of brick and concrete offices are dotted about the yard wherever space can be found for them. Other than for its BR re-roofing, the depot changed little from 1938 until closure in July 1967.

Below: As the setting sun paints the wheel rims and motion of Bulleid 'West Country' Pacific 34018 *Axminster* in burnished gold in the late afternoon of 28th October 1966, 'Merchant Navy' class Pacific No 35013 *Blue Funnel* has come off a Waterloo – Bournemouth express at the west end of the station, and has set back on to the up through line before running forward on shed. No 35013 will coal and join the light Pacific that had arrived a few minutes earlier, which is now on the ash pit road. The procession of engines to and from shed was one of the delights of a visit to Bournemouth Central, though not so welcome to the residents in the houses immediately next to the shed, and a prominent Southern Region sign commanded 'QUIET PLEASE RESIDENTIAL AREA'.

Above: A grimy 'West Country' Pacific No 34093 *Saunton* coals at Oxford GWR shed on 30th October 1965. The Bulleid light Pacific has come up with an express from the Southern Region, and has handed it over to be worked on via the Great Central. Coal wagons, one of which is on the elevated line on the right, were shunted up an inclined ramp into the coal hole, and their contents emptied on to the floor of the coal hole, where it was shovelled into a trolley which the coalman is pushing on to the hinged ramp visible above the tender of No 34093. The curved ends of the ramp prevented the trolley going too far and landing in the tender! The contents were tipped into the tender, and the whole laborious process

repeated until the tender was full. Unlike the LMS and LNER, both of which invested in mechanised coal plants at important sheds, the GWR did not, preferring to build new coal holes as at Oxford. The Oxford coal hole, which was built in concrete blocks and buff brick, rather than the red brick of earlier structures, dated from 1944, and had replaced a decrepit timber edifice. The reason for this 'backwardness' was that Great Western engines were designed to burn South Wales steam coal. This is a soft friable coal, and is more likely to break up than the harder steam coals used by the northern companies. If South Wales coal is subjected to the rough treatment of a mechanical plant and dropped from much

greater heights, it is likely to go to dust, making it less suited to locomotive use. The GWR reasoned that any savings in manpower at the coal hole would be eroded by higher fuel consumption on the road. Engine crews would often rake out their fires whilst waiting to coal, and piles of clinker were a common adjunct to the coal hole.

Below: LMS and LNER engines were designed to use poorer but harder northern steam coal, and both companies accepted damage to coal as the inevitable price of mechanised coaling. By the late 1930s, many large LMS motive power depots had received concrete coaling plants. One surprising installation was at

Belfast (York Road), the headquarters of the LMS/NCC. The Midland Railway had purchased the Belfast & Northern Counties Railway in 1903, renaming it the Midland Railway, Northern Counties Committee. It became the LMS/NCC in 1923. In 1931, Malcolm Spier, a 44 year old LMS officer with an outstanding war record that included the MC and three mentions in dispatches, was appointed Manager & Secretary. Always hard-up for money, the NCC was archaic and dispirited, but Spier was to transform it, one remarkable achievement being to persuade the parent LMS to fund the reconstruction of York Road locomotive depot in 1935. A new 60 foot powered turntable was supplied, along with an LMS standard No 2 coaling plant, both of which appear in this view taken on 30th August 1964. A wagon hoist lifted loaded coal wagons up the inclined rails at the right of the coaling plant and tipping them bodily to discharge the contents into the concrete hopper. The track layout was reorganised, so that an engine arrived, took water, turned and took coal. Loco sand was available near the coaling plant. The loco moved to the ash disposal plant, and after that went on shed or in traffic. When a second smaller coaling plant was opened at Coleraine in 1938, locomotive coaling over the whole of the NCC was concentrated at two depots with

significant economies. It was a textbook example of sound management. The locomotives here include NCC No 2, a class WT 2-6-4T, which became the NCC 'maid of all work', operating everything from expresses to coal trains. Next to No 2 is a former Sligo, Leitrim & Northern Counties 0-6-4T, UTA No 26 *Lough Melvin*, which was acquired second hand by the Ulster Transport Authority when the SL&NCR closed in the 1950s. Sister engine, No 27 *Lough Erne*, which was later preserved, is visible to the right of the picture.

Above: The Great Northern Railway (Ireland) operated over 600 route miles, and its International status after the partition of Ireland secured its independence until the 1950s. The GNR(I) was hard hit by partition and the Depression, and although a progressive company that introduced diesel railcars before the celebrated GWR railcars, it was handicapped by lack of funds. One line diverged from the Dublin – Belfast main line at Portadown, and ran via Omagh to Londonderry. This route was always referred to by enthusiasts and railwaymen alike as the 'Derry Road. The approach to the city was along the banks of the River Foyle, and the GN terminus was named Foyle Road to distinguish it from the other three termini in the city. The

locomotive shed was just outside the station on the banks of the River Foyle. No doubt, the GN would have liked to improve its facilities, but cash resources were not available. The assets of the GNR were divided in 1958 between the two nationalised railway operators on either side of the border, lines in Northern Ireland passing to the UTA, and right up to closure of the 'Derry Road' in 1965, locomotive ash was dumped on the ground outside the shed, the ash later being shovelled into an open wagon for disposal. UTA No 35, formerly GNR No 41, an SG3 class 0-6-0 goods built by Beyer Peacock in 1921, simmers gently amongst the ash heaps at Foyle Road on 1st September 1964. The red 'D' on the cab side is a power classification, from which the engines gained their nickname of 'Big Ds'. The locomotive is in grimy UTA lined black livery, with the UTA coat of arms on the tender. This was one of the few railway heraldic devices to receive official sanction from the College of Arms. Locomotive ash being truly international, this view, with its three foot high ash heaps, should be of help to modellers who want a really convincing environment for their motive power depot.

Top: After coaling, watering, cleaning their fires and turning, engines would either go back into traffic, or on shed to receive routine attention, a boiler wash, or minor repairs. No words can recapture the atmosphere of a large steam shed but the sounds and smell of steam, hot oil, and engines raising steam, lives on in the memory of all who knew it. Then there were the visual effects. The shadows from the glazing bars on the roof, the smoke ducting and the girders that held the roof created a living tapestry, whilst the beams of light that pierced the atmosphere replicated the beams of lights shining down from a theatre or cinema. Engines on Rugby No 1 shed in July 1964 included an Ivatt class 2 tank, a Stanier 8F, a Stanier Mogul and 'Black Five' No 45448, but it is the atmosphere that matters. Rugby was one of the many northlight sheds built by F W Webb, CME of the LNWR. The idea of the saw tooth profile northlight roof is to admit light without admitting too much heat from the sun. The shallow angle is clad in slate, corrugated iron or other material, whilst the sharply inclined angle is glazed. This faces north if possible, and east or west, if not. It never faces south. As with many of Webb's products, including signal boxes and lever frames, 'Cauliflower goods' or 'Jumbo' 2-4-0s, it was a neat job intended to function efficiently at the minimum cost. The shed replaced earlier Northern and Southern division steam sheds, and was a part of the transformation of Rugby station between 1876 and 1886. Built as two adjacent 12 road sheds, No 1 shed was rebuilt in 1955 with a corrugated iron and glass roof, whilst No 2 shed was demolished in 1960. It was a straight shed and was a victim of dieselisation and electrification of the West Coast Main Line, closed on 25th April 1965.

Left: Although Rugby had a population of over 50,000 people, it had but one depot. Keith, which is midway between Aberdeen and Inverness, had a population of 4,000 people and *TWO* engine sheds. Keith was at the boundary between the Great North of Scotland Railway to the south-east, and the Highland Railway to the north-west. The Great North of Scotland Railway reached Keith in October 1856, and provided a four-road stone shed with arched entrances. It was rebuilt in 1954, when steel joists replaced the original arches, and the local stone above the gables was replaced with brick. The tracks had been lifted shortly before I took this view of Keith shed on 9th July 1969. Fifteen years after its rebuild, the replacement brickwork still looked new. It was later converted for industrial use. The Highland Railway arrived in 1858, and also provided a four-road stone shed with arched entrances, but was halved in size in 1868, when part of it was moved to Blair Atholl. Both sheds survived until nationalisation, but with few engines at Keith, BR transferred all work to the GNSR shed, and closed the HR shed. Few modellers would have the space for Bournemouth or Rugby sheds, but the two small sheds at Keith are practicable, and the continued existence of both until nationalisation would make Keith an interesting prototype for the modeller.

Right: The 'straight shed' with a row of parallel tracks reached off an approach fan, was the most common type, but the Midland, the GWR, the North Eastern and other companies also built roundhouses, where the shed roads radiate off a turntable. Two basic types existed. In one type, the turntable was open to the sky, and the tracks radiated off the turntable into covered stalls or bays. In the other type of shed, the turntable and the entire fan were under cover. Staveley shed, which was renamed Barrow Hill after nationalisation to avoid confusion with the ex Great Central shed of the same name, was fully enclosed. It was a standard Midland roundhouse opened in 1870, and despite its 'roundhouse' name, was actually rectangular. One problem with such roundhouses is that stabling roads are very short. With the Midland small engine policy, this was not a worry before 1923, but gave the LMS problems at some sheds later on. This was not the case at Barrow Hill, as many of its allocation were shunting engines under a contract for a 100 year period entered into between the Midland Railway and the Staveley Coal & Iron Co in 1866. As a result of this astonishing deal, Midland 0-4-0Ts, the celebrated Johnson 1F 0-6-0Ts, and a couple of BR/Kitson 0-4-0STs shunted Staveley works until October 1965, and even then were retained in stock until the agreement expired the following year! Midland 0-4-0T No 41528, is at rest in Barrow Hill shed on 24th July 1964. The class, a Deeley design, originated in 1907 when five engines, Nos 1528 to 1532, were built at Derby. Five more engines appeared in 1921/22. The shortness of the shed roads and the inspection pits merits study, as does the fire devil and the nondescript office on the right.

Below: The traditional route for the footplate man was to start as a cleaner, picking up knowledge from instruction classes and contact with engines. In due course he would progress to passed cleaner, who was passed to work as a junior fireman on shunting engines. As he gained firing experience he would become a fireman, working through the links from shunting engine to express passenger turns. He would be tested and if competent, become a passed fireman, who was passed to do junior driving turns. He would progress through the links again. By the 1950s, it was difficult to recruit staff for the unsocial hours and hard work of a cleaner, and vacancies often went unfilled. Locomotive cleaning suffered, and by the sixties, 'engine grime' was the normal livery. On 22nd July 1964, my father and I were shown round Southport shed by the shedmaster. Southport-based No 44767, the Stanier 'Black Five' with outside Stephenson link motion, had been booked for a railtour, and the shed master had put all his cleaners to work to polish up this unique locomotive. The back of the tender, the tender frames, and the smokebox still needed work, but otherwise No 44767 was in superb condition. Apart from the engine, the discarded loco spring in the foreground, the heaps of ash and the fire devil to keep the water columns from freezing up in winter, are typical shed yard clutter. The chairs are of the two hole pattern, as loco yards were often products of the pre-grouping era and were low on the agenda for relaying.

Opposite page top: When an engine was ready to go back into traffic, the fire lighter would check that the boiler had been filled with water and use old sleepers and kindling wood to light up. Sometimes the shed pilot would pull it out of the shed, or it might move off shed into the open air as soon as it had sufficient pressure to move. The reason for getting it outside is apparent from this view of No 7821 *Ditcheat Manor*, at Banbury on 20th September 1965. As engines raise steam, they produce clouds of choking yellow-black smoke, and the sooner they are out of the shed, the better it is for anyone working in the building. At this stage, the tender will be piled high with coal, and the driver and fireman will be arriving soon. Water columns such as this GW design, with its operating valve handle, fire devil, swing arm, bag and pull chain to swing the heavy arm round so the fireman can put the bag in the tender, were a feature of the shed fan at any steam depot.

Opposite page bottom: The crew have oiled round No 6815 *Frilford Grange*. The tender was piled high with coal after she came in off her last duty. She would also have been filled up with water, but some will have been used in lighting up. As a final step before going into traffic, the driver and fireman are topping up with water. When I first studied this slide, I thought that No 6815 would be leaving Oxley shed tender first, but if so, she would carry the light engine head code, which is one lamp on the lamp bracket above the coupling. I then realised that this could not be the head code,

as one lamp over the near buffer had been discontinued under the 1962 head code revisions, when the class 'J' coal or mineral train that had carried that code, was merged with the class 'H' unfitted through freight, sometimes known as an 'up and downer', from its code of one lamp at the base of the chimney, and one above the coupling. The lamp is the tail lamp, with its red aspect, but it has not yet been lit, so is indistinguishable from a headlamp. Oxley shed, visible in the background, was a standard two turntable GWR roundhouse, and was opened in July 1907. No 6815 is on the northern exit road from the far shed which loops around the left of the near shed and plunged diagonally through a hole in the side wall to reach the turntable. For much of its life, Oxley, although having a larger allocation that the nearby Stafford Road shed, was overshadowed by its neighbour with its 'Counties', 'Kings' and 'Castles' used on the Birmingham main line expresses. Stafford Road closed in September 1963, its remaining top link power migrating to Oxley to join the 100 plus mixed traffic, freight and shunting engines that Oxley had traditionally looked after. Oxley itself closed in March 1967.

Above: Apart from engines belonging to the main line railway companies, there were several thousand steam locomotives in industrial use. Four or six coupled saddle tanks predominated from the mid-nineteenth century to the 1960s, by which time the demise of heavy industry, dieselisation, and the shift away from rail transport was thinning the ranks of

the survivors. The smallest industrial systems might consist of two or three sidings, and have hardly enough work to keep an engine and crew occupied for a single shift, but elsewhere the scale of operations could be very different. The biggest post-war user of industrial steam was the National Coal Board, which still operated over 600 collieries in the early 1960s, most of which were rail connected. The NCB was divided into administrative Areas, one of the busiest being the Northumberland Area, with over twenty pits and coal preparation plants managed from its headquarters at Ashington, which was itself a busy colliery with its own motive power depot and the Area locomotive workshops. Over 30 steam locomotives were still in stock in the late 1960s, along with a growing fleet of diesel shunters. One diesel, and no less than eight of the Area's steam engines are visible in this view of the loco depot and its environs at Ashington in April 1968. Engines that can be identified include Nos 47, 41, 6 and 27. No 6 was a wartime Bagnall delivery (Bagnall No 2749 of 1944), whilst Nos 41 and 47 were part of a large batch of engines provided by Robert Stephenson & Hawthorns in the 1950s.

TUNNELS

Even though we live in an age when speed is commonplace, the 'whoomph' when the train we are travelling in enters a tunnel is still dramatic. If we go back to the dawn of the railway age, what must it have been like for our forebears, whose standard of speed had been a galloping horse ? We cannot imagine the awe and fear that they felt, and when locomotives were prone to failure, and the time interval system prevailed, that fear was justified, for an accident that might be trivial on the open line, could become a catastrophe within the confines of a tunnel. Thankfully, such accidents have been few, but they show that a tunnel is a fearful place if things go wrong. As modellers, we like to see our trains, so burying them in a tunnel seems pointless, but a tunnel can be invaluable to us. In real life, there is no boundary between the real world and the fiddle yard, but in model form there comes a time when our tracks must 'exit stage'. Two of the best ways to achieve that transition are by the use of overline bridges, or a tunnel.

Above: Clouds of smoke belch from the tunnel mouth, as No 44685, a Stanier 'Black 5', bursts out of the south portal of Kilsby tunnel on a summer excursion on 7th August 1964. Even today, Kilsby would be a formidable engineering challenge, but in the 1830s, this 1 mile 666 yard long tunnel, pushed technology to the limit. It is on the London & Birmingham Railway where a high ridge crosses the Midlands south of Rugby. Robert Stephenson was the engineer, and to allay the anxieties of passengers, the tunnel mouth was 28 feet high and 25 feet wide. Quicksand and water were encountered, and the contractor, who was faced with ruin, gave up in despair, and later died. With a crisis looming, Stephenson took over, employing direct labour. With 13 pumping engines extracting 1,800 gallons of water a minute, it took a year and a half to subdue the flooding and cost £300,000, or three times its estimate. Once completed, the London & Birmingham was opened throughout on 17th September 1838. The tunnel received a major overhaul in 1953, including a new drainage culvert, a full relay and chipping away a century of mineral deposit from the tunnel lining. The deposit was 'as hard as steel' as one of the tunnel gang remarked, and because of its multi-coloured and wrinkled appearance 'like a crocodile's

back', was much in demand for local rockeries! In the 1950s and 60s, my father exhibited several sections of the O gauge layout he was building. The final layout was 28 feet long. To to mask the transition to the fiddle yard, he used Kilsby tunnel. He had an on-line permit from the District Operating Superintendent for the area, and with official permission, took the necessary measurements, and photographs.

Opposite page top: In the 1960s, there was a spoof article that BR were to build additional 'Castle' class 4-6-0s from No 7038 onwards, and that names would include *Elephant & Castle* and *Barbara Castle* (a prominent Labour MP of the day). My father suggested that *Kilsby Castle* would be even better, as it really did exist. If you look on the map, you will not find such a castle, but if you join the Watling Street at Kilsby village and head south, you will see a crenellated red brick tower on the left hand side of the road. In order to speed up construction work on the tunnel, and to admit light, two sixty foot diameter ventilation shafts were driven down from the high ground to a depth of 90 and 120 feet. Smaller ventilation shafts were provided at frequent intervals. Once the tunnel was completed, the two main shafts were built up with these towers, partly as an expression of pride in the tunnel, but primarily to prevent anyone falling down the shaft. Inevitably the local people dubbed the tower next to the road 'Kilsby Castle', so Robert Stephenson built a Castle some 85 years before the first Collett 'Castle' of the GWR!

Bottom: In September 1986, we revisited Kilsby Tunnel. The most obvious change was the introduction of internal lighting. They reveal that unlike some tunnels where the mouth is of greater diameter than the bore, to deceive passengers as to the size of bore, Robert Stephenson retained the same generous dimensions throughout. A 25 kv electric locomotive is approaching the north end of the tunnel on an Up express. In surveying the portal, my father noticed the strata lines in the stone. The grain can be pronounced or light, and horizontal or diagonal. He reproduced this pattern block by block. Few modelling aids were then available, but he found that the wood from a marquetry kit was ideal. (Marquetry is the art of creating patterns using thin pieces of differently coloured wood cut to size). Most modellers make two mistakes in producing a tunnel. In real life, engineers do not deliberately find a small hummock to drive a tunnel through, but on many layouts the tracks make a beeline for the only rising ground on the layout. In reality tunnels exist where a railway faces a major obstacle, not a hummock. If we look at Kilsby the ground slopes up each side of the tunnel mouth. The second problem is that modellers level the ground off immediately above the portal. If by digging out another two or three feet of soil, the engineer could use a cutting, he would do so. At Kilsby, the ground rises over 80 feet above the tunnel mouth.

Above: The Great Grimsby & Sheffield Junction Railway was incorporated on 30th June 1845 to build from Gainsborough to Grimsby via Kirton-in-Lindsay, Barnetby and Brocklesby. It was absorbed into the Manchester Sheffield & Lincolnshire Railway on 27th July 1846. John Fowler was appointed engineer to the GG&SJ, the contractors being John Stephenson & Co. Fowler, later Sir John Fowler, was born at Sheffield in 1817. His first experience as resident engineer was on the Stockton & Hartlepool Railway in 1839. In 1844, he set up as a consulting engineer in London, the GG&SJ being one of his first clients. His later work included the Metropolitan Railway and the Forth Bridge. There were two major civil engineering works on the GG&SJ. The first was the bridge over the River Trent at Gainsborough. The second was the 1,325 yard long Kirton tunnel, which was north of Kirton Lindsay station. It was built in red brick with decorative towers with arrow slits and narrow round headed windows each side of the bore, giving it a distinguished appearance. The line opened from Gainsborough to Grimsby in 1849. Kirton tunnel is depicted in 1989, at which time the line through Kirton Lindsay was under threat of closure.

Opposite page bottom: I secured this interior view of Kirton tunnel during an engineers' inspection, the unusual angle emphasising the egg shaped bore, and the cutting through which the railway runs, before plunging into the tunnel. If the modeller intends to build a tunnel to disguise a curve from the scenic world to a fiddle yard, there is a pitfall for the unwary. As modellers, we use sharper curves than the prototype. As a result the overhang at the front of a large locomotive is greater than in real life, whilst the overhang of the centre of a bogie coach is greater than on the prototype. If we build a tunnel to scale dimensions on a curve that is sharper than the prototype, a large locomotive or bogie stock may foul the tunnel walls, or may foul one another on a double track tunnel if the track separation is not increased. It may be necessary to increase the dimensions of the tunnel. It is not ideal, but is one of the compromises we must sometimes accept.

Below: We associate the Great Eastern with the flat fens, yet in places the ground is anything but flat. Ipswich provides a wonderful prototype for the modeller. The ground has been cut away to provide space for the station, so the tracks come together immediately beyond the platforms, and the line plunges straight into a ridge without an approach cutting. The Eastern Union Railway was incorporated in 1844 to build a 17 mile line from Colchester to Ipswich, and opened to a temporary terminus south of Stoke Hill in June 1846. Meanwhile the Ipswich & Bury Railway was building a 26 mile route to Bury St Edmunds. The two lines were to be joined by a 361 yard long tunnel through Stoke Hill. The I&B opened to passengers on 24th December 1846, trains reversing in and out of the EUR station. Both lines had several directors in common and were engineered by Joseph Locke. The I&B was absorbed into the EUR in 1847, but it was not until 1860 that the present

station was opened on the north side of the tunnel. Class 86, No 86 230 *The Duke of Wellington,* is starting away from the platform en route to Colchester and Liverpool Street in May 1990. My father felt that the Ipswich scenario, with the line plunging into a tunnel within yards of the platform end offered great scenic possibilities. For the modeller, the trees and bushes that grow above the tunnel mouth provide a convenient way to increase the apparent height of the ground above the tunnel mouth without making the terrain slope too steeply.

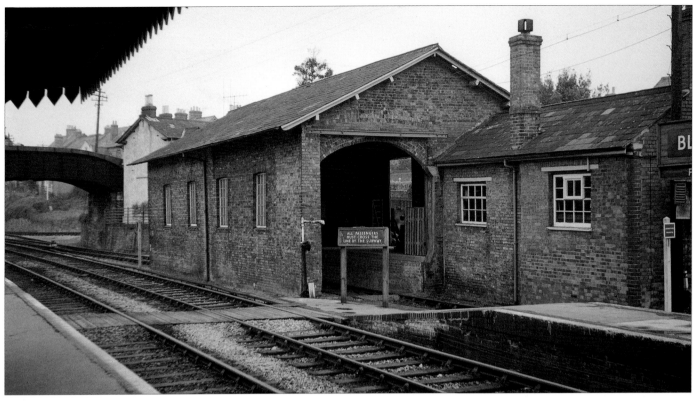

GOODS DEPOTS

We have looked at passenger-only stations ranging from New Hadley to Glasgow Central. Here we will study a classic passenger and freight station, and some goods depots. This was a world where the public seldom ventured, nor were they welcome, due to risks to the unwary that could occur during shunting operations and the possibilities of theft.

Above: Blandford Forum was midway between Templecombe, where the Somerset & Dorset Railway connected with the LSWR, and Wimborne on the original LSWR route to Bournemouth. The Dorset Central Railway reached Templecombe from the south on 1st November 1860. In 1862, the Dorset Central and the Somerset Central Railway formed the Somerset & Dorset Railway, and completed the link between Blandford and Templecombe on 31st August 1863. Poor returns led to a take-over by the MR and LSWR, the route being known thereafter as the Somerset & Dorset Joint Railway. Blandford Forum (population 3,600), was the largest community between Wimborne and Templecombe, giving an idea of the rural nature of the area. The goods yard included a small brick goods shed off the end of the down platform. A side loading dock existed north of the footbridge, but the cattle dock and a six ton crane were in the main yard. To cope with larger rolling stock, the goods shed doors were widened, weakening the arch, which was strengthened by a length of rail bolted to the brickwork. We visited Blandford Forum on 12th April 1966, just after passenger

services had ceased. Freight continued to be handled at Blandford until 6th January 1969.

Opposite page top: Nottingham, a city of over 300,000 people, has long been a centre of lace manufacturing, bicycles, pharmaceuticals and tobacco. The MR, the GNR and the GCR all served the city, whilst the LNWR had an isolated goods depot, reached via running powers over the GN. Of the four companies, the Midland was dominant, its line running east-west about 200 yards south of the Nottingham Canal. The MR goods depot was on the site of the Midland Counties Railway terminus in Nottingham, which faced Carrington Street, and opened on 30th May 1839. In 1844, the MCR was absorbed into the Midland, whose Nottingham - Lincoln extension opened on 3rd August 1846. This began 26 chains west of the terminus, so through trains arrived at the MCR station, and then backed out, to go on to Lincoln. This was inconvenient, so a new through station was opened on 22nd May 1848 on the Lincoln line east of Carrington Street. The MCR station became the Midland goods depot. The six-story British Waterways goods warehouse reminds us that the Nottingham Canal flanked the MCR terminus. Although we think of railways as killing the canals overnight, this was not so, as the canals carried lower value freight where speed was not important until well into the twentieth century. Of the 30 or so major canals vested in the Waterways Executive of the BTC, almost half came from the Railway Executive, including the 14¾ mile Nottingham Canal, which had been GNR property. Although prominently lettered BRITISH WATERWAYS, traces of an earlier railway title are visible. The double doors on each floor permit goods to be lifted from the narrow boats to the warehouse

by hoists. Railway warehouses followed the same design, so this building would be an ideal backdrop in a large railway goods depot. The platform and canopy on the left and the end loading docks are typical. The seven-story warehouse on the right reveals how goods depots developed piecemeal over their working lives.

Opposite page bottom: In this portrait of the Midland yard taken on 6th July 1976, Nottingham Goods Yard East shunting frame occupies the foreground. Flat roofed yard cabins like this controlled movements to and from freight running lines, but not the hand points in the sidings, and were common in large LM Region yards by the 1960s, but have largely vanished, as traditional goods depots have become industrial estates or shopping malls. The clutter by the door, including a seat, shovel and tail lamps would add character to a layout. The two-story MR goods warehouse still bears a weathered LONDON MIDLAND AND SCOTTISH RAILWAY BONDED WAREHOUSES title. If manufacturers had to pay the very high excise duties on cigarettes as soon as they are produced, it would tie up a vast amount of capital long before any income came in. The 'bonded' warehouse was a secure building, where H M Customs & Excise had agreed that goods could be stored without any duty being paid until they were sold to retailers, and left the warehouse. At cities such as Nottingham, where cigarette traffic from the John Player factory was heavy, the railways provided bonded warehouses in return for the tobacco companies consigning goods by rail. Numerous lamps provide light for shunting by night. A row of BR shock vans shows that the yard is still busy, as do packing crates and other items scattered about the yard.

Above: The LNWR branch from Coventry to Nuneaton was authorised on 3rd August 1846, and opened on 2nd September 1850. Coundon Road station was a short distance out of Coventry, on the north side of the level crossing over Coundon Road, and became engulfed in the spread of the city. Passenger services were withdrawn between Coventry and Nuneaton on 18th January 1965, and Coundon Road station closed. Through services later resumed, but Coundon Road was not re-opened to passengers. An eleven-road goods yard, Coundon Wharf, which was primarily for coal, and could hold about 330 wagons, was built south of the station, between Coundon Road and Holyhead Road. No facilities for end or side loading, or cattle were provided, and general freight facilities were withdrawn on 30th November 1964, the station becoming a coal concentration depot. This portrait of Coundon sidings on 3rd June 1971 shows the grouping of the sidings in pairs, the wide space between each pair of tracks for lorry access, the coal heaps and the coal stockades made from old railway sleepers.

Opposite page top: The first chauldron wagons on the early railways were horse drawn, and whilst the 'iron horse' displaced the equine variety from train duties, horses continued to shunt in goods yards and passenger stations, and for cartage, taking goods, parcels and luggage to and from the stations. In 1913, the railways' 27,826 cartage and shunting horses

outnumbered locomotives! On 1st January 1948, BR inherited 8,793 horses, of which 8,555 were cartage horses and 238 for shunting. In the first year, BR purchased 532 new animals, but in the unique entry relating to horses, 1,719 were 'sold or died during year', a net drop of over 1,000 horses in one year. The association between railways and horses ended in February 1967, when the last shunting horse was 'withdrawn' at Newmarket. We talk of engines being stabled at a shed, but the 'iron horse' borrowed the word stable from its living counterpart. Stables varied from a single stall at a country station to a block accommodating hundreds of animals, as with the GWR Mint Stables at Paddington, which was three stories high, with inclined ramps connecting the different levels. Most stables were single storey with louvred ventilators on the roof, although railway arches were also used, if the line was carried on a viaduct. Otherwise the stable block was near the perimeter of the goods yard. At Rugby, the LNWR stables adjoined Wood Street, and survived until June 1991. The unkempt grass is railway property. Until the 1970s, railings separated it from the road. The chief signal fitter at Rugby, a keen model engineer, got permission for a short track between the railings and the stables. Miniature steam locos puffed up and down, taking excited children for short rides. This would make a wonderful prototype for the modeller in 4 or 7mm using a Z gauge loco with an automatic control.

Opposite page bottom: As with the steam engine on its return from duty, the horse needed servicing when it finished work. If the horse was sweating, it was dried off, as it could catch a chill or even pneumonia, which was very serious in a stable. The harness was hung up on pegs by the entrance to the stall. Although harness for working horses was not tailored to an individual animal, it was adjusted to suit a particular horse, so it was important not to mix up horses and tack. The horse was then led head first into its own individual stall, as the provender rack was at the inner end of the stall. The age of the railway horse ended in 1967, but in one place, the association between horses and rails survived. This was at Douglas, in the Isle of Man, where horse trams had clipped along the promenade since 1876. As at Paddington, the stables were multi level, with ramps connecting the levels. In a busy and well run stables, where horses went on and off work at different times, a competent horse keeper or head farrier would arrange that animals on early shift would be grouped in one stable, and those on later shifts in another stable. This was to avoid disturbing the rest of the animals that were off duty when other horses came in or out. This is the 'night stable' at Douglas, where the horses on late turn were kept. Although stables were kept clean, the horsey smell plus droppings that had not yet been swept up made the stable a smelly place, though the railway horse tended to work in better conditions than many other horses.

LEVEL CROSSINGS

Level crossings were a bone of contention between the railways and the public from the start. Opponents claimed that the noisy steam monsters would frighten the horses, and be a scene of death and destruction. In the United States and on the Continent, people were expected to show common sense, and if they did not, it was their bad luck. In Great Britain, railways were seen as dangerous things, and rather than allow road users and railways to meet, fencing and gates were essential. Horses quickly adapted to the railways, and whilst foolhardy pedestrians were run down, gated crossings virtually eliminated collisions with road vehicles, because the horse, which is inherently sensible, had no desire to smash through or leap over big white gates. The policy succeeded, but was inherently rigid and slow. Opposition switched to the delays to vehicular traffic, and the danger to impatient pedestrians. By the end of the nineteenth century it was very difficult to gain parliamentary approval for lines that crossed busy roads on the level. The price extracted for new railways or major rebuilding of existing lines, was the inclusion of footbridges and road bridges. The frequency of level crossings on any route is a good indication

of its age. Old lines and old stations had them, and if they were not drastically altered, retained them. New lines did not, and had stations such as Lincoln or King's Lynn, both of which had notorious level crossings, been built in the 1890s, rather than at the dawn of the railway age, bridges would have been demanded. The gated Victorian crossing survived into BR days, but the installation of lifting barriers, which, unlike gates, could be automatic, or controlled from a remote signal box, and the Beeching closures have diminished its ranks. In the following pages, we will look at a variety of traditional gated crossings.

Above: The 'ideal' level crossing, if such a thing exists, is where road and rail cross at right angles, and both are the same width. Four equal length gates will then fully close against the road or the railway, depending on where they are set. In the real world, this may not happen. At Swinderby, which is midway between Newark and Lincoln, the MR crossed a narrow country lane at a sharp angle. Double track lines and narrow roads are bad news, and when you add an awkward angle, it gets worse. The primary function of gates is to stop a road vehicle driving on to the line in front of a train, so the priority is to block the roadway, when a train is approaching. In some places a four-gate crossing is provided, and the gates have to be shut in the correct sequence, as they overlap one another when closed against the narrow opening. An alternative is to build gates that

will block the roadway, and accept that they are not long enough to fully close off the railway. This applies at Swinderby, where the left hand gate closes against the railway, but the right hand gatepost is so far from the track that even when the gate is shut against the railway, it is nowhere near the track. The cabin is a Midland type 3a design of 1901, and houses a 16 lever frame. It is an interesting but messy solution.

Opposite page top: In the early days of railways, the time interval system prevailed, so crossing keepers had no clear idea of when trains were approaching. The normal position of signals was off, and signals were put to danger for 5-10 minutes after the passage of a train. Given this operating system, and the light road traffic, it made sense if crossing gates were normally closed AGAINST the road. If a horse drawn vehicle came along, the crossing keeper put his signals to danger, opened the gates, let the cart by, and closed the gates again. As the volume of road traffic grew, this became unpopular, and with the adoption of signals normally standing at danger, and only being cleared for the passage of a train, no longer made sense, but many years elapsed before the BoT decided that gates should ordinarily be shut against the railway. In a few places, where a minor lane crossed the line, the old system survived. One such location was Rolleston Junction. The RING BELL FOR GATES notice and push button warn the motorist that this crossing works in the way that was usual one hundred and fifty years ago. After the motorist has rung the bell, the crossing keeper checks that no trains are in section between Fiskerton box to the west and Staythorpe Crossing to the east. If the line is clear, he opens the gates and beckons the motorist across. Although gates normally open against the railway at a public level crossing, Rolleston is operated in the same way as an occupation crossing, i.e. the gates open away from the railway line. The only time that the crossing carries much road traffic is when Southwell Races are running. A private occupation crossing to an old mill and the race course exists north of the station, and on race days, a man with hand signals and detonators was provided on the Down line ¾ of a mile west of the Station House crossing, and another man, similarly equipped, stood ¾ of a mile east of the Mill Crossing. Their duty was to shoot every train with a detonator, and display a yellow hand signal. The crossing keepers were to display a red hand signal when the gates were open to road traffic, and a green signal after they had been closed.

Below: Hartlebury is on the GWR between Kidderminster and Droitwich, and was the southern end of the triangle that gave access to the Severn Valley Railway, the northern connection running in to Kidderminster, and now being part of the popular preserved railway. When I first visited Hartlebury in July 1976, the junction box was closed, but the station box was celebrating its centenary, and still contained a mechanical frame, which was replaced by a small panel in 1982. The level crossing was at right angles, and road and rail were of comparable width, so the crossing was fully closed by four equal length gates. The crossing gates are interlocked with the signals, so must be closed against the road before the signals are cleared. As the signalman will want to clear his distant, the train will be a considerable distance away when the crossing is closed. To avoid delaying pedestrians, small wicket gates are provided at many crossings. At Hartlebury the platforms adjoin the crossing, so pedestrians use the footbridge rather than wickets. The road is made of crossing timbers rather than tarmac. They can be easily lifted for maintenance work, so were less inconvenient than tarmac.

Left: Where a secondary line crossed a little used road, crossing gates were usually opened by hand, as at Launton, as it was simple and cheap. On important lines, or where the road was busier, a gate wheel was common. When he wants to close the crossing, the signalman checks that the road is clear and turns the wheel. A small diameter toothed gearwheel is connected to the axle, and turns with the big 'ship's wheel'. This moves a toothed rack, which is connected by point rodding to the gates. The signalman can open all four gates simultaneously without leaving the box. This is good for him, and it is much quicker, and facilitates efficient train working. Once the gate wheel has been turned, the gates are locked in position from the frame and the signalman can then pull off for the train. With the steady replacement of level crossings by barriers, the gate wheel is becoming rare, so this illustration will help modellers to detail the interior of a box working a level crossing. The gate wheel is always at the end of the box facing the crossing, so that the signalman has a good view.

Below: The Boston, Sleaford & Midland Counties Railway was authorised in August 1853 to build a line from the Great Northern Railway at Boston to the GNR at Barkston, near Grantham. It opened in two sections, the Sleaford-Boston portion being completed in April 1859. It was worked by the GNR from the outset and absorbed in 1864. Heckington was the first station east of Sleaford. The main buildings at Heckington are on the Down platform, and although out of railway use, retained their character when photographed in June 1994. A level crossing gate is very long for its depth, and this puts considerable strain on the top beam of the gate. Most companies built strength into their gates by dividing them into panels with a vertical post, and diagonal or 'X' struts, and horizontal iron tie bars. The GNR provided a taller gatepost, and added a third hinge, from which a tie bar ran to the base of the gate. This offered more triangulation, and added greatly to the strength of the gate. The single tie rod split into two flat steel straps just above the top rail of the gate, one running each side of the structure. It complicated assembly of the components as great precision was necessary if the gate was to open freely, but it was a sound design, especially if the entire width of the line was to be covered by one gate, rather than two short gates.

Right: This portrait of the crossing at Heckington and the adjacent windmill is a rural idyll. The twin bracing straps run to the penultimate panel of the gate, rather than to the very end, whilst the hinge castings from which the gate is hung, go through the entire width of the concrete gate post. As is common on crossing gates, the horizontal tie rods pierce the wooden diagonals at an angle, making for a very strong structure, but one that is very difficult to model. The use of appropriate wayside structures is as important to the modeller in locating a layout geographically as getting the railway buildings right. Today we live in an era of standardised buildings, but until the start of the twentieth century, local building traditions predominated. The mellow golden brown stone of the Cotswolds is particularly well known, but in the north of England, granite and limestone are common building materials.

Below: Boat of Kintore Level Crossing, seen on 4th July 1969, is 13 miles north of Aberdeen on the Great North of Scotland Railway between Inverurie and Dyce. Long ago, travellers on the road from Kintore to Hatton crossed the River Don by boat nearby, hence the name. Because of the abundance of good quarrying stone in the district, GNSR buildings were created using a mellow grey-brown or silver-grey granite. The GNSR was in a parlous financial state in the nineteenth century, so was behind its neighbours in signalling the system, but early boxes were mostly of stone with a hipped roof. Boat of Kintore is unusual as the base is of rough dressed granite, whilst the top is of locally produced brick. The windows, are not the sliding type usually found in signal boxes, but are centre pivoted. The gates are unusual. Instead of wood or concrete gateposts, the posts are iron. Instead of the usual 'X' pattern timber bracing, the GNSR has divided a long gate into two panels, with one diagonal timber running upward from the joint by the bottom hinge. Instead of round targets, they are diamond shaped with white edging. Two tie rods run from below the diamond to a strain block that is inclined at an angle.

Opposite page top: Until 1843, Folkestone was a small fishing port, with narrow cobbled streets dropping down steeply from the high ground to the seashore where the boats landed their catch. The arrival of the South Eastern Railway at a temporary terminus to the west of the town on 28th June 1843 put Folkestone on the railway map. A few months later, the SER engineer, Sir William Cubitt, completed the 19 arch Foord viaduct which soared 100 feet above the narrow streets of Folkestone to carry the railway over a steeply graded valley that lead down to the harbour. The Folkestone to Dover section was completed on 7th February 1844. The harbour had been built by Thomas Telford in 1809, but had not been a success, and was purchased by the SER in 1843 as a port for the company's own Channel packets to France. Despite steep gradients and sharp curves, the SER started work on a branch that would run down the valley to the harbour. Whilst this was completed within a few months, five years elapsed before it was opened to passenger traffic on 31st December 1848. It was 1,328 yards long, with a drop of 111 feet between the Junction and the Harbour, and because of the severe grades and restrictions on motive power, up to four engines were needed to take boat trains to the Junction. In less than a mile, it included a couple of level crossings, a fixed bridge and a swing bridge. For part of its length, The Tram Road, as the highway to the west is known,

paralleled the branch, whilst Dyke Road ran to the east. Two roads crossed the harbour branch on the level, Folly Road, and East Cliff. We are looking from Dyke Road to The Tram Road and East Cliff on 10th June 1973. As with the GNR, the South Eastern have braced these gates with diagonal tie rods from a third hinge, but in the SER design the tie rod extends to the end of the gate. The painting style on the red target also merits attention.

Opposite page bottom: Perhaps the most improbable scenario you could invent for a model railway would be to have a level crossing and a road bridge parallel to one another, and just a few yards apart. It would look totally unprototypical, so it is a pleasure to show that the Southern made this error! We are standing on East Cliff crossing, and looking downhill towards Folkestone Harbour. Just a few yards from the crossing, a concrete viaduct carries Radnor Bridge Road above the line. From the junction to the harbour, where the tracks level out, the gradient is a constant 1 in 30, which is steeper than the legendary Lickey incline. The South Eastern and its bitter rival, the London, Chatham & Dover Railway formed a joint operating committee in 1899. Although remaining separate legal entities, the new South Eastern & Chatham Railway Companies Managing Committee ended the fierce rivalry that had so harmed both companies, to their mutual benefit.

Below: The most remarkable crossing gates I have seen are in Ireland. Rathmore is on the single track branch from Mallow (on the Dublin to Cork main line) to Killarney, which was built by the Killarney Junction Railway in 1853. In contrast to the Hull & Barnsley, one of the most costly lines in the British Isles, the KJR cost less than £5,000 a mile, making it one of the cheapest lines ever built. It was taken over by the Great Southern & Western Railway in 1860, and amalgamated into Great Southern Railways after the partition of Ireland. In 1945, it became Coras Iompair Eireann, and is now Irish Rail. Rathmore signal box, with its cement rendered walls, is an unexciting structure, but the gates, if that is the right word, are amazing. The gatepost is tubular steel with a conical cap. The hinge post is timber with top and bottom iron caps that act as the bearings on which the gate swings. The 'gate' consists of two horizontal timbers that diverge from one another for the first third of their length, at which point there is a cross beam. They run parallel for a short distance, and then come together at the far end of the gate. To prevent this beam sagging, tie bars run from the upper hinge cap to the beam. Wire mesh is hung from the beam, as is a rectangular white target with a red cross. A vertical beam at the far end of the gate, with a pair of diagonal arms for triangulation, helps to keep the mesh in place. Access to the signal box is off the landing of the green painted footbridge.

BRIDGES

The first bridge in the world must have been a tree trunk that had blown down and fallen over a river. Early man discovered it was a convenient way to cross the water, and the transition to a man-made bridge was a small step. The tree trunk bridge obeys the same rules of physics as the most modern prestressed concrete girder bridge. The weight rests directly on the abutments, and as the span increases, the load that can be carried decreases, until the bridge will collapse as a man, horse or train crosses it. Early man would have found out the hard way. One answer was a bigger tree trunk, but the limit of what is feasible is soon reached.

Another answer is the arch bridge. Gravity attracts everything to earth, whether it is an apple or a brick, but the ancients discovered that if a series of tapered stones are arranged in a semi circle with the narrow end of the stone facing downwards, and the ends of the arch restricted from moving outwards, gravity is defeated.

Gravity still attracts each stone to fall to earth, as the weight of the bridge and any load, whether it be man, cow or engine, presses down on the top of the arch, but the central stone, known as the keystone cannot fall out, because it is wider at the top than the bottom. Unless an adjacent stone is removed, the keystone is supported by the neighbouring stones on each side. They, in turn are supported by their neighbours. The forces exerted by gravity in trying to make the stones fall down are redirected outwards along the lines of the arch. At the end of the arch, it is necessary to support this load. This is the purpose of the piers of a multi-arch aqueduct, or the abutments on a single arch bridge. If the foundations on which the pier or abutment rests are inadequate, or if it is too weak to support the load transmitted to it by the arch, it will fail, permitting the arch to deform and the bridge will collapse.

The classification of bridges is a study in itself. The overline bridge carries something over the top of the line. An underline bridge carries the line over something. A bridge carrying one railway over another, is an overline bridge for one route, and an underline bridge for the other line, and is called an intersection bridge. There are arch bridges and beam bridges. To take beam bridges, they could be a wooden beam, or plate, box or lattice girders. Lattice bridges could be divided into many different types. The variety is breath taking, and would take many volumes to explore. However, bridges are of interest to the modeller as they offer superb scenic possibilities and convenient ways to mask the transition from the modelled world to the fiddle yard. They also offer pitfalls to the unwary. Bridge design is complicated, and even the professionals get it wrong at times. The most celebrated railway bridge to fail was Bouch's Tay bridge in 1879. In 1940, American engineers got it wrong with the Tacoma Narrows road bridge, and a cameraman was on hand to film the bridge disintegrating in a 42 mph wind less than five months after it had opened. Modellers also make mistakes, and invent bridges that would have collapsed during construction. In this section, I have covered a range of traditional bridges, showing a variety of constructional features, materials and purposes, but with ten times the space, one could only scratch the surface.

Opposite page: The Romans created bridges and aqueducts that have survived for 2,000 years, and built a network of military roads that ran straight as a die. One such road was Watling Street, and because of the lie of the land, they routed it through a low lying gap in the ridge that traverses the south Midlands, which was later called the Watford Gap. It is a few miles south of Rugby, and not to be confused with Watford Junction. When the Grand Junction Canal was built from the Oxford Canal at Braunston to London, it used the Watford Gap, as it was the most sensible route. A few years later, Robert Stephenson tramped over the same ground, and selected the Watford gap for the London & Birmingham Railway. The 'wheel came full circle' in the 1950s, when the designers of the M1 used the same narrow corridor through high ground. 86 256 *Pebble Mill* races south with an Up Euston express at Buckby Wharf in September 1986. The shadow of the M1 bridge can be seen through the arch of the Stephenson bridge. It is a classic semi-circular arch bridge with heavy abutments on each side and buttresses to give further strength. It also reveals that with a semi-circular arch, the height of the arch is equal to the radius of the curve, i.e. half the diameter of the span. As the distance to be spanned grows, the height of the bridge increases. Where the distance to be

spanned is small, this is not a problem, but to cross a river on a 100 foot span, an arch 50 feet in depth is needed, which requires costly embankments.

Above: The Romans knew they could omit the lower portion of a semi-circular arch, if the ends of the segment that remained were adequately supported. On a segmental arch, the direction of force is at the same angle as the last stone in the arch, that is, downwards and outwards at a shallow angle. This necessitates a massive abutment to support this angled load. If these forces exceed the strength of the abutment, it would tip over backwards, causing the bridge to collapse. Apart from mastering the segmental arch, bridge builders dispensed with costly tapered stones. With mortar to hold bricks in place, a much cheaper arch could be made by placing a row of bricks on end, adding a little more cement at the top of the bricks to create a taper effect. Early segmental arch bridges omitted only a small part of the semi circle, but as experience was gained, engineers adopted a segment from an arch of much greater radius. The angle of thrust at the end of the segment was even shallower, imposing a greater strain on the abutment to tip over backwards, but provided this was allowed for, it would permit a wider arch relative to its height. This brick segmental

arch bridge carries the MR over Stratford Street North near Camp Hill goods station in Birmingham. The arch consists of seven rings of brick, and rests on a massive bedstone, or skewback, the outer face of which is shaped to meet the arch at a right angle. Subsidiary segmental arches take footpaths on each side of the road. A vertical brick wall with fill behind it is prone to collapse outwards, so the wing wall inclines backwards. The area of brickwork between the arch and the parapet is referred to as the spandrel. The parapet wall above the bridge is topped with long coping stones, and modern cable ducting has been clipped to the outside of the parapet. When I took this view on 1st June 1971, the pavements on each side of the road were of traditional paving bricks, rather than the 'twee' modern paving bricks that the town planners spew about today. Except for the cars, this scene would have hardly changed in decades, giving added value for the modeller.

Opposite page top: The elliptical arch also achieves a wide span without excessive height. The radius of an ellipse changes in a smooth progression, being sharpest at the ends and its most gentle at the middle. In bridge building work, the depth of an elliptical arch will be about half that of a semicircular arch. This delightful elliptical arch masonry bridge supports the GER line from Cambridge to Bury St Edmunds and Ipswich in the vicinity of Thurston station. The bottom of the abutments are quoined, whilst a row of projecting bricks or dentils provide decoration beneath the cornice from which the arch springs. A further row of dentils appears below the parapet. At first sight, the arch is not symmetrical, but this is an optical effect caused by the angle of the photograph and because the road is on an 'S' bend, creating a slight skew effect. Although the bridge carried height warning triangles, giving the maximum permissible clearance at the centre and the side of the arch, the brickwork and the 12 foot clearance sign have been struck by a road vehicle. If this damages the integrity of the arch, which seems to be the case, it can affect the stability of the bridge. A major strike could bring a bridge down. Some pipes project from the spandrels. Ideally the upper surface or decking of the bridge should be waterproof, but some water will seep into the structure, and this could affect its stability, so run-away pipes are provided to allow trapped water to escape. The platforms of Thurston station start on the right hand side of the bridge, and a length of tubular steel fencing has been provided to prevent unwary passengers falling over the bridge parapet.

Opposite page bottom: Albrighton station is on the Shrewsbury & Birmingham Railway, which was part of the GWR route from Paddington to the Mersey. The section from Oakengates to Wolverhampton opened on 12th November 1849, and after a prolonged battle with the LNWR, was absorbed into the GWR in 1854. At Codsall and Albrighton, the platforms extended over the adjacent roads, and were supported by shallow cast iron beams. These bore the inscription THOMAS PERRY & SON 1848 HIGHFIELDS FOUNDRY. A decorative cast iron parapet reinforced by five ornate pillars tops the beams. Cast iron is strong in compression, i.e. squashing, but has little ability to resist tension, e.g. stretching or bending. It is no longer acceptable for bridges carrying trains, but for platforms is permissible. Cast iron also has advantages, for unlike steel, which loses strength through corrosion, cast iron is all but impervious to corrosion. A potential drawback with cast iron is that due to the stresses set up as the casting cools down, stress lines may radiate out from any corners. A good iron master arranged that castings had curves, tapers or fillets where there was a corner. The curved mouldings on the parapets on this bridge at Albrighton, which was photographed on 1st July 1976, are not purely for decoration. The running lines are carried on deeper plate girders that can be seen in the shadows beneath the bridge.

Above: At Syston, just north of Leicester, the Midland main line made a triangular junction with the Syston & Peterborough route. The junction was controlled from three boxes, and we are looking from the North box towards Syston South Junction in June 1973. Syston South Junction box is to the right of the rear most coach of the Down express, which is hauled by D100 *Sherwood Forester*, a type 4, later Class 45. The freight train is on the sharply curved chord to Syston East Junction. This view shows what a plate girder underline bridge looks like from above. The girders on the face of the bridge are the visible part of a structure, that includes cross girders to support the decking, track work and ballast, and intermediate longitudinal spans as well. The Midland main line was originally double track, and was later quadrupled, so what appears to be one four-track bridge, is actually a pair of double-track bridges. An intermediate girder exists between the Up and Down fast lines, but two girders appear between the fast and slow lines. One span is for the fast line bridge, and the second span, which is separated from it by a few inches, is the outer span of the slow line bridge. The girder next to the freight stock is the intermediate span for the slow line bridge. Nowadays welding is common for steelwork, but in the past a girder consisted of steel plates that were riveted together. The ends of a girder can be square or it can curve down. In building a bridge, the modeller should consider the history of the line, as an 1830s arch, as at Buckby Wharf, would be wrong on a line built in the 1890s. On the other hand, a modern bridge could appear as a replacement on an early line. Whether intermediate girders on an underline bridge should be square ended or round ended is best decided by examining other photographs of a particular company's practice at different times.

Above: In the previous section, we visited East Cliff level crossing on the Folkestone Harbour branch. The original Telford harbour of 1809 was square in shape, and in 1844, the South Eastern Railway built a short pier out into the centre of the harbour. The harbour branch tracks extended on to the pier, and permitted convenient exchange of freight and mail, but the line was not authorised for passenger traffic for another five years, so passengers were conveyed to and from the pier by horse drawn omnibuses. The SER realised that the tidal harbour was too small for the vessels they planned for the cross channel services, and opted for a new harbour station on the seaward side of the Telford basin. For this to be rail served, the line had to cross over the inner harbour. A fixed bridge would obstruct shipping, so a swing bridge was installed in 1847 to connect the harbour branch with the new passenger station, which opened in 1850. It was one of the first railway swing bridges in the world. The SER replaced the original swing bridge in 1893, and the Southern installed the third bridge on this site between 10th and 12th May 1930. The bridge was under the control of the Folkestone Harbour Station Master. Before

opening the bridge, no Up or Down trains were to be in section, and the signalman at the Harbour signal box had to give the Blocking Back signal to Folkestone Junction which would prevent any train being offered down the branch. The bridge was controlled by bridge bolt locks, one on each side. They were operated from the box, and once they were out, the running signals at the harbour were locked. The bridge could then be swung for shipping to pass through. The drawback of having steel structures in close proximity to the sea is rust, as this September 1974 study of the bridge reveals.

Opposite page bottom: The Cheshire Midland Railway opened between Altrincham and Knutsford in 1862, but hoped to extend to Chester. It was absorbed by the Cheshire Lines Committee the following year, and in 1874, the CLC finally reached Chester. Delamere, with a population of under 700 even in the 1950s, is a mile south of Delamere Forest, and midway between Chester and Northwich. The station is in a sylvan location next to the forest, where a segmental arch bridge carries the B5152 Frodsham to Delamere road over the line. It is built in dressed red sandstone. Rather than a brick arch, the spandrel walls are supported by large tapered stones called voussoirs. The Roman bridge builder Vitruvius, who was writing in the first century BC, said of Voussoirs that, 'their joints are directed to the centre', that is, if you extend the lines of the joints, they would meet at the centre of the arch. Vitruvius knew that tapering the stones so that the joints were radial was vital to sound bridge building, but cared little whether the lower faces, or intrados, were left rough, trimmed to the circumference of the arch, or cut straight, as they had no structural function. At first, the Romans cut the upper faces, or

extrados, to the circumference of the arch. When the spandrel wall was of large blocks of stone, it was difficult to joint the horizontal blocks against the curved extrados. The Romans then adopted the pentagonal (five sided) voussoir, in which the upper faces are shaped so they will be vertical and horizontal when they are in the arch. Pentagonal voussoirs are used on this bridge, which was photographed in 1989. The modeller can create voussoirs by marking a centre on a sheet of foam board, and lightly drawing a series of pencil lines radiating from the centre to the extrados of the voussoirs. When the individual stones are scored into the board, the sides will taper as Vitruvius explains. Using the centre, a curve can be scored marking out the bottom of the stones or intrados. For a four-sided voussoir, the extrados, or uppermost edge of the voussoirs is scored in the same way. For pentagonal voussoirs, horizontal lines are lightly marked on the foam board to define the stone courses. The radial lines of the voussoirs will intersect the horizontal lines of the stone courses. Short vertical lines need to be marked out at the intersection points. If you study the photograph, the desired result is obvious. The structure in the background is part of the Verney aqueduct taking water from Lake Verney to Liverpool. Decorative brick abutments on both sides of the line support three parallel 3ft 6in diameter pipes. No arches or other support is required as a tube forms a very strong structure capable of carrying a substantial weight by itself.

Below: Disguising the transition between the modelled section and the fiddle yard has always presented problems. The combined efforts of nature, the LYR, the LMS and BR produced a perfect answer in Liverpool. Nature's contribution was in the geology of

Merseyside, with a low-lying area on the bank of the Mersey into which the docks and commercial properties that made up the heart of Liverpool were crammed. High ground lay within half a mile of the waterfront. The LYR Exchange terminus faced north, and served three busy routes. Leaving Exchange on a continuous viaduct, the LYR line divided at Sandhills, the Southport line taking the easily graded coastal strip to Southport. The quadruple track main line, now joined by up and Down freight lines, continued for half a mile to Kirkdale West, where a connection trailed in from the Liverpool docks. Kirkdale station, nestling in a deep cutting, lay between the West and East boxes. At the east end of the station, Westminster Road crossed the line by a three arch bridge, the arches taking from left to right the goods lines, slow lines and fast lines. Access to the station was via steps from Westminster Road at its junction with Marsh Street. BoT rules provided that no flight of steps was to exceed 10 feet without an intermediate landing, and three landings were required at Kirkdale. A plate girder footbridge ran from the intermediate landing to the booking office. The freight lines ended beyond Westminster road, the quadruple track cutting continuing on to the twin bores of the 210 yard long Kirkdale No 2 tunnel, and beyond that to the 497 yard long Kirkdale No 1 tunnel, before splitting at Walton Junction for Preston and Manchester. Between Westminster Road bridge and Kirkdale No 2 tunnel, a lattice footbridge crossed the line. The combination of a circular arch bridge, a high spandrel wall and parapet, and the visual disruption provided by the plate girder footbridge creates a perfect scenic break.

Below: At Cheltenham (Lansdown), on the MR Birmingham to Bristol route, Gloucester Road crosses the line on this skew girder bridge, which was photographed on 1st July 1976. The girder consists of a vertical plate or web, which is secured to the top and bottom flange plates, by angle iron and rivets. The angle iron and rivets securing the angle to the bottom of the web are visible on the left. Angle iron or T section vertical stiffeners are riveted at to the web for added rigidity. A gusset plate is riveted to alternate stiffeners, and to the top and bottom flanges. The rectangular groups of rivets, which are arranged in pairs in a 3, 2, 3 pattern between the stiffeners, secure the cross girders (that support the roadway) to the web by angle plates. To save weight, the heavy web plate is no deeper than necessary, so the parapet that stops people falling off the bridge is usually separate. It can be of brick, iron, steel or timber. Although the plate will be lighter, this parapet is built in the same way as the structural girder with a web, top and bottom flanges and stiffeners. Alternate flanges carry a gusset to hold the parapet upright. The girder rests on a bedstone, which will be of stone or concrete and is absolutely level and flat, so that the weight of the bridge is spread evenly over the abutment. To allow for expansion and contraction, one end of the bridge is fixed, whilst the other end is free to move. As the weight is transmitted down through the ends of the girder, an additional gusseted stiffener is provided on the span above the left hand bedplate. The bottom two layers of stone in the abutment have not been dressed, but have been left rough. As the bridge crosses the line at an angle, it is a skew bridge. On a bridge, the cross girders run at right angles to the main girders. On a skew bridge, this means they do not run at right angles to the abutments. The absence of rivets shows that cross girders are not attached to the two left hand panels of the main girder, as they would serve no purpose.

Opposite page top: Many different beam bridges evolved. In the bowstring bridge, a curved top chord joins the bottom member at both ends just as the ends of an archer's bow are connected by the bowstring. The hogback bridge, which is often confused with a bowstring, also has a curved upper member, but this is separated from the bottom boom by uprights at the end. This example is on the City of Dublin Junction Railway, which strides across the heart of Dublin, connecting the Amiens Street (now Connolly) terminus of the former Great Northern Railway (Ireland) with the Westland Row headquarters of the one-time Dublin & South Eastern Railway. The line, which was financed by the GNR(I), the Dublin, Wicklow & Wexford Railway (a predecessor to the DSER), and the City of Dublin Steam Packet Company was a vital artery in Ireland's rail network, and carries the busy DART or Dublin Area Rapid Transit trains today.

Opposite page bottom: The plate girder is a simple beam bridge, but bridge builders realised that the forces of compression and tension acted on the top and bottom of a beam, and in some way, diagonally as well. In theory, material can be omitted from parts of a beam that do not carry any forces without compromising strength. With the advent of railways, bridge building developed rapidly. In its original form, the Warren truss of 1848 was composed of equilateral triangles, whilst the lattice beam consisted of top and bottom members connected by diagonal bars crossing one another at right angles. They used between 67% and 73% of the material of a plate girder. However, the theory was not fully understood. At a meeting of the Institution of Civil Engineers in April 1855, Robert Stephenson commented; 'The comparison between plate and trellis bridges is a subject of great interest, and deserves the best consideration of the Institution. The introduction of beam bridges on railways has imposed on the profession the necessity of considering the true nature of the beam, and the strains to which it is subjected, when supporting a weight, and consequently the laws by which it resists those strains.' Stephenson preferred the conservatism of the tubular bridge or plate girder, to the openwork or trellis girder. As much of his work has endured for a century and a half, his opinion must be respected. On the other hand, another brilliant engineer, G P Bidder, commented,

'The real saving consists in the economical use of materials in the vertical web'. It could be built of plate, or as an openwork beam. At Royal Oak, half a mile out of Paddington, the Metropolitan Railway's 'Hammersmith & City' line platforms lie between connections to the GWR goods and passenger stations, and are crossed by the two-span Ranelagh bridge. This is a heavily braced hogback bridge, trussed on the later Warren principle, which differed considerably from early Warren trusses. The centre section in a Warren truss is an X between vertical members if there are an uneven number of sections, but if the bridge is divided into an even number of sections, the two centre sections are formed this way, as the span must be symmetrical. On the rest of the span, the diagonals slope away from the centre. The use of three 'X' sections is unusual, but in a span divided into 15 sections, retains symmetry.

Opposite page top: If you ask people to name the most famous bridges in the world, the Sydney Harbour bridge, the Golden Gate in San Francisco, and the Forth railway bridge would head the list. They are no longer the biggest or the newest bridges in the world, but their hold on popular imagination is unchallenged. Why is this? The Forth Bridge was the culmination of the 'Bridges Route' up the east coast of Scotland from Edinburgh to Aberdeen. The work was initially entrusted to Sir Thomas Bouch. His Tay bridge had opened to much acclaim in May 1878, but collapsed in 1879, carrying a trainload of people to their deaths. It was a national humiliation, and a replacement bridge that opened a few years later was only a partial expiation. A new triumph was needed. Sir John Fowler and Sir Benjamin Baker, joint engineers to the Forth Bridge, provided that triumph when the Prince of Wales, later King Edward VII, opened the bridge on 4th March 1890. An arch bridge, a girder bridge or a suspension bridge, even if they are of great length with repeated spans, are simple to look at. The Forth Bridge is big, and whether you view it close up, or at a distance, it is not simple. A riot of tubes soar skywards, and whilst the onlooker is sure they all do something, what they do is a mystery, and mystery adds to enchantment. Most bridges are painted in quiet colours, but the Forth Bridge is red. This was not showmanship, but because a vast steel structure rusts, and the best protection was red lead paint. Nowadays lead paints are banned, but their protecting powers were unequalled in Victorian times, or even today. Finally, the painters start at one end of the bridge, and by the time they have reached the far end, it is time to start all over again. When a bridge erases a nation's humiliation; when it is big and mysterious, and when you paint it bright red, it is not surprising that it is special. When my father took this view from one of the car ferries that used to ply across the Forth on 25th July 1962, the road bridge that now spans the Forth was some years in the future. To grasp the size of this structure, look for the trains. A southbound train is dwarfed by the near cantilever. A northbound train is about to enter the far cantilever. When a full sized steam engine weighing over 100 tons is reduced to insignificance, it tells us a lot.

Opposite page bottom: In the general view of the Forth bridge, the approach spans were reduced to insignificance by the massive cantilever sections, and few enthusiasts pay attention to them. In any other setting, a lattice span of 168 feet would rank as a major bridge. In this scene, taken on 25th July 1962, a Gresley A3 Pacific is dwarfed by the 'insignificant' part of the bridge. When my father screened this view over 40 years ago, he said it was a shame we could not read the number of the engine. Many years later, I noticed that whilst it is an A3, the smoke deflectors were not the standard German batswing deflectors applied by BR. They were similar to the deflectors on the Thompson and Peppercorn pacifics. However they lack a

nameplate, and other details are wrong for the later designs. I realised that there was only one candidate. No 60097, *Humorist*, was used by Sir Nigel Gresley for smoke lifting trials in the 1930s, and had received these unique deflectors. By sheer chance, we had photographed a unique engine. From December 1961, and until her withdrawal in August 1963, No 60097 was based at Edinburgh St Margarets. The coal rails of the GN tender stand out clearly against the cloudless blue sky. Whilst few enthusiasts will attempt to model the Forth Bridge, this view provides detail for the modeller who wants a lattice girder bridge on his layout. The pier is gracefully tapered and the joint between the two spans that rest on the pier is apparent. The lower booms, are connected by lattice cross girders and diagonals as well. The contractor to the Forth Bridge was William Arrol who was born in 1839, and began life repairing porridge pots. He passed away in 1913, after a glittering career that included the replacement Tay bridge, the Forth Bridge and Tower Bridge, and a knighthood on the day the Forth Bridge was formally opened.

Below: This study of the base of the piers was taken on 20th July 1959. The bridge consists of three double cantilevers formed of steel tubes and girders, the cantilever sections being connected by suspended spans. At the north,

or Fife side, the bridge is approached by five girder spans and three arches resting on masonry piers, with ten spans and four arches on the south or Linlithgow bank. Each cantilever rests on four masonry piers that rise 18 feet above high water level. Steel bedplates which are secured to the piers by great bolts provide the anchorage for the inclined tubes or 'skewbacks'. These 12 foot diameter columns, which are built of ⅝ inch thick steel plate, rise 330 feet above the piers. More tubes connect the skewbacks on the same side of the bridge at the base and apex. A spider's web of lattice girders connect the tubes transversely across the bridge. The cantilever portions contain 51,000 tons of steel, whilst the central towers of the cantilevers are 120 feet wide at the base, tapering to 33 feet at the top, as is apparent here. The surface area of the steelwork is 145 acres, and the bridge was designed to withstand a wind pressure of 56lb per square foot, or 2000 tons on each of the large spans! To put the size of the bridge in perspective, if you built an O gauge model of the bridge, it would be over eight feet tall. Ignoring the approach spans, it would be 64 feet long.

ENGINEERING DRAWINGS

In preparing for the parliamentary battles to secure a railway act, civil engineers produced thousands of outline drawings, which would be worked up into fully detailed plans prior to awarding construction contracts. Alterations might be required during construction, and once the railway was open, drawings were still needed in profusion. In many cases they were hand coloured. This was to aid clarity, but meant that many nineteenth century engineering drawings were works of art, as well as working documents. Loss of records in the Blitz during the Second World War, closures of old railway drawing offices and the destruction of unwanted files in the modern business environment has seen thousands of irreplaceable drawings lost, but surviving examples are a fruitful source of information for the modeller. This section reproduces selected items from Victorian times.

Page 91, Stour viaduct,
Oxford, Worcester & Wolverhampton Railway
The OW&W was called the Old Worse and Worse. Sadly, the title was merited, as it was a dreadful railway. It was allied to the GWR, and when authorised in 1845, its chief engineer was Isambard Kingdom Brunel. His estimate for the 89 mile line was £1.5million, but over-optimism and additional demands by parliament pushed the likely costs to £2.5 million before construction began, and it got steadily worse. Funds were slow to come in, and the OW&W repeatedly tapped the GWR for money, and played the gauge card, flirting with the LNWR and the Midland. Relations with the GWR soured, and Brunel resigned as chief engineer. The Droitwich to Stourbridge section opened on 1st May 1852. North of Stourbridge, the OW&W crossed the River Stour on a wooden trestle. The BoT was dubious about this and other trestles, and although the Stourbridge to Dudley section opened for freight in November 1852, authority to carry passengers was withheld until 20th December 1852. Brunel's superb trestle bridges became a hallmark on the lines he engineered. They rested on generous masonry bases, with soundly designed uprights and a generous radial fan to support the decking, and lasted for decades. The trestles on the OW&W were very different. Instead of masonry pillars rising to half or two thirds of the height of the bridge, one base was just 5ft tall. Instead of wooden beams or iron tie rods connecting the tops of the pillars some 30ft below deck level, where the wooden supports fanned out from the top of the masonry base, the tie beam was 14ft 3in below deck level. The fan was correspondingly short and left a greater length of deck unsupported. One trestle of 12ft x 12ft timbers towered up 57 feet without any bracing. Even Brunel's prototype trestle of 1837, which carried the Bath road over the GWR at Sonning

cutting (and not the weight of a train) was more robust, as the legs were angled to provide triangulation. Although Brunel had surveyed the OW&W, and no doubt planned a trestle, it is hard to believe he designed this bridge. It was probably slimmed down after his resignation in response to the company's financial plight. An early illustration shows how spidery and frail it was, a far cry from the well-engineered Brunel trestles. The GWR took over the line, and by 1875 decided that all the OW&W wooden trestles needed replacing. A ten span masonry viaduct appeared in 1882. Interestingly the preliminary design is lightly pencilled in on this plan.

Page 92, Bridge 21,
Denbigh, Ruthin & Corwen Railway
The Denbigh, Ruthin & Corwen Railway was authorised in July 1860, and opened from Denbigh to Ruthin on 1st March 1862, and to Corwen on 6th October 1864. It was in the 'no man's land' between the LNWR on the North Wales coast and the GWR at Llangollen and Bala. Bridge No 21 between Ruthin and Eyarth, was on the southern section of the DR&C. The GWR, keen to reach the north coast, offered to lease the line, but negotiations collapsed. The LNWR obtained powers to work it, but this fell through. The contractor ran it, and went bankrupt. The DR&C then operated its own services before collapsing. It was next worked by the LNWR, and absorbed in 1879. Passenger services ended in 1953 and freight ceased in 1962. On 2nd February 1888, Crewe prepared this plan to rebuild the 1863 bridge No 21, using second hand cast iron girders lying at Northampton. This reveals a system whereby materials could be recovered from old bridges where they were no longer adequate, and transferred to places where they were sufficient. The roadway is carried on four longitudinal hog backed girders. They do not have top and bottom flanges of equal dimensions, but a 4in top flange, which is in compression, and a 12½in bottom flange, which is in tension. Cast iron is strong in compression, but weak in tension, so the asymmetrical girder puts the 'meat' where it is most needed. Small brick arches, called jack arches, between the longitudinal girders provide an arched or vaulted base for the roadway. This was common with overline bridges. To secure the girders during construction, they are drilled and held together by 1¼in iron tie rods. The abutments are of stone with bedstones of a hard wearing material. The equally spaced vertical lines on the elevation of the parapet wall indicate a vertically planked wooden parapet, whilst further lines reveal the external framework to which the planking was secured. Such parapets are rare today, but in 2002, we found a bridge on an abandoned line with a similar wooden parapet. A double track bridge was often provided on a single line in the hope of future growth in traffic. Re-use of materials in this way can sometimes result in materials that are 'out of period' appearing on a line, which may be confusing for the historian, but can be convenient for the modeller!

Page 93, Cocker viaduct,
Cockermouth, Keswick & Penrith Railway
General George Armstrong Custer had a glittering career with many victories. He is remembered for the battle he lost, at the Little Bighorn. Sir Thomas Bouch built many railway bridges. He is remembered for the Tay bridge, which collapsed when a train was crossing it in 1879. There were no survivors. Custer lost his entire force, and became a national hero. Bouch was pilloried by the engineering establishment and died in disgrace. When I was a child, my parents took me by train from Keswick to Penrith. It was a fantastic trip through the heart of Lakeland. Many years later, I realised that the engineer who built that line was Sir Thomas Bouch. Sadly it is now closed, but it outlived its creator by over 60 years. The Cockermouth, Keswick & Penrith Railway commenced at Cockermouth Joint station, crossing over a small lane and the River Cocker at the station throat. Bridge No 8 was designed by Bouch, and was built in 1864. It was a segmental three arch masonry bridge, and carried the Up and Down loops which merged on the far side of the river. Connections from the Up sidings joined the Up loop on the viaduct itself, which tapered from three to two tracks. With growing traffic and industrial development on the far bank of the river, Cockermouth station was enlarged in 1881-82. The work included widening the original viaduct to three tracks throughout, the third track providing better access to the private sidings and acting as a headshunt for cattle pens behind the Up platform. The contract was let to Fleming & Murray in 1882. The enlargement was to the same design as Bouch's original work. The scale plan shows how the piers were extended on the north side of the line, and how they were keyed in to the original masonry. Bouch had a reputation for building railways through difficult terrain at low cost. He was undoubtedly brilliant, but in his desire to keep costs down, he was inclined to build too lightly. The shallow spandrel wall above the arch of the Cocker viaduct demonstrates this tendency. Many Roman bridges, such as the Ponte Fabricio in Rome, have equally shallow spandrel walls, and have stood for 2000 years, but they did not have to take the weight of a steam locomotive. The LMS rebuilt the bridge with reinforced concrete beams in 1944-45.

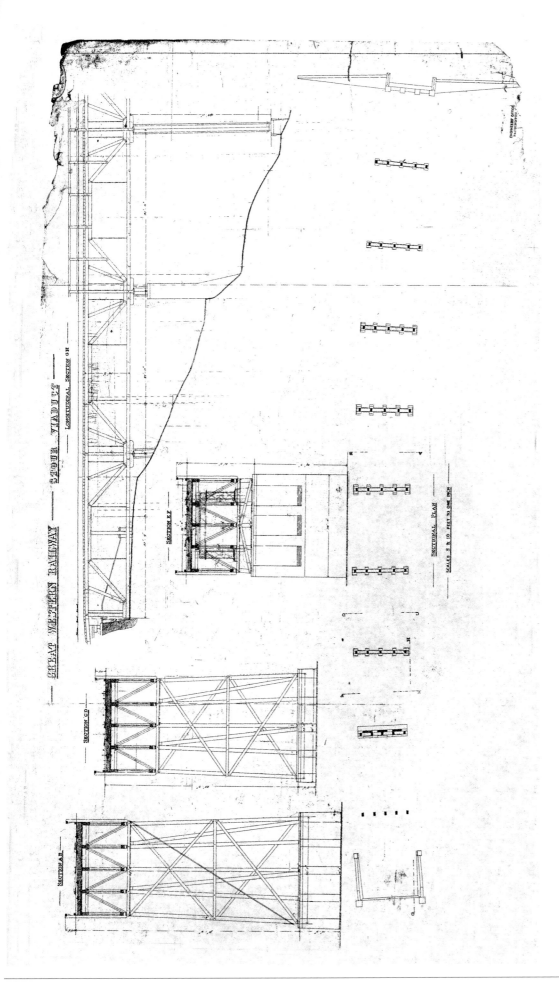

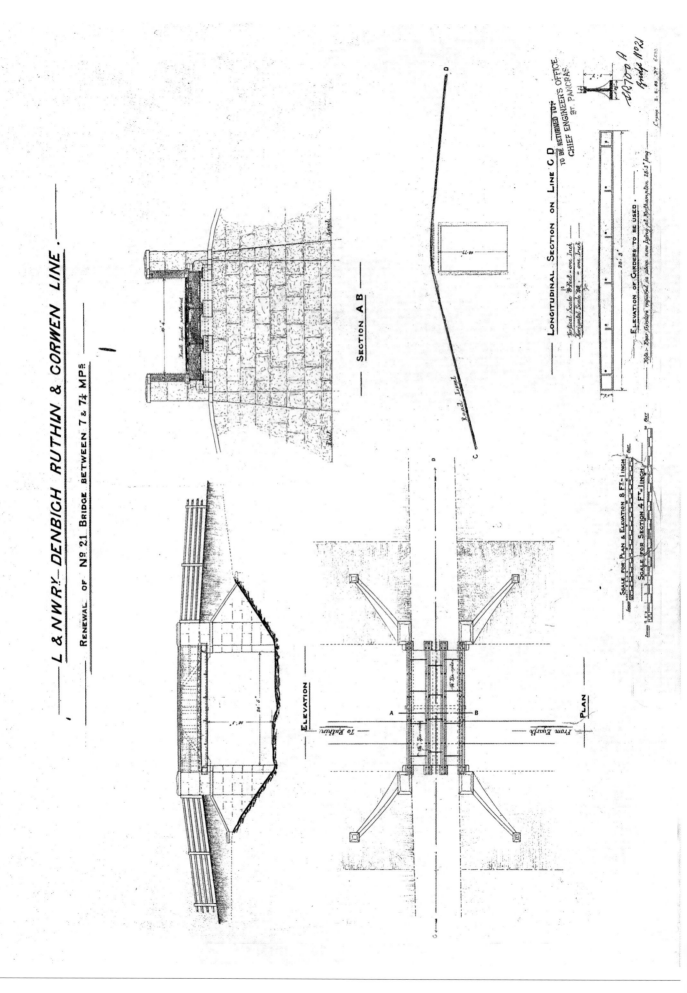

— L & N.W.R.Y.- DENBIGH RUTHIN & CORWEN LINE. —

— RENEWAL OF Nº 21 BRIDGE BETWEEN 7 & 7¼ MP.ˢ —

SECTION A B

LONGITUDINAL SECTION ON LINE C D

Vertical Scale 8 Feet = one Inch
Horizontal Scale 54 = one Inch

ELEVATION OF GIRDERS TO BE USED

ELEVATION

PLAN

SCALE FOR PLAN & ELEVATION 8 FT = 1 INCH

SCALE FOR SECTION 4 FT = 1 INCH

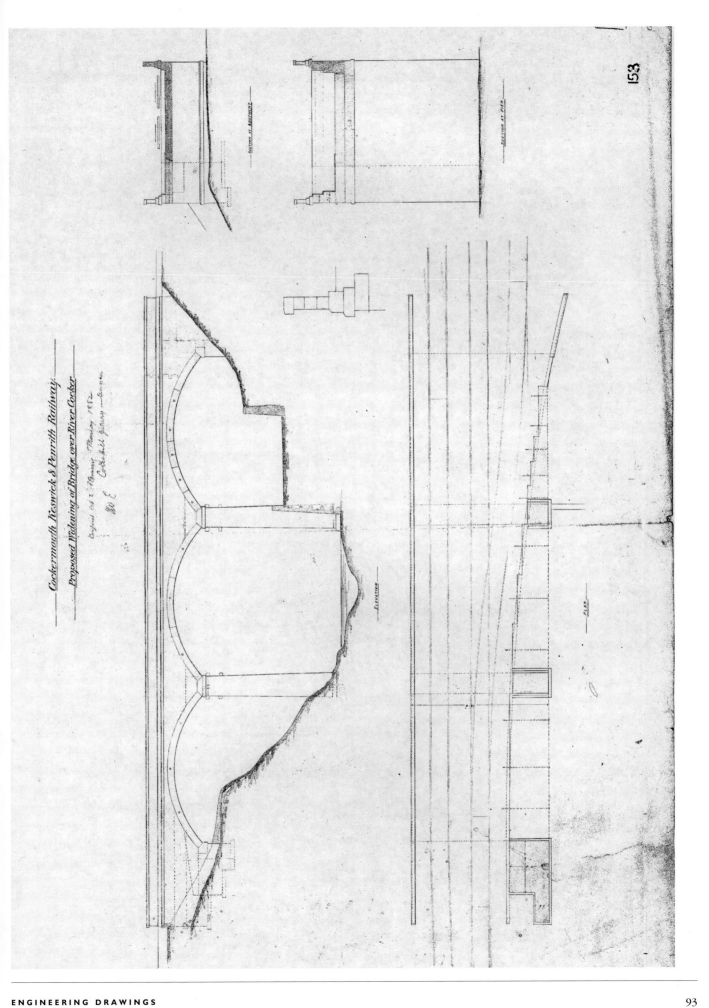

BoT REQUIREMENTS

The Board of Trade issued regulations for the construction of new lines or fresh work at existing stations, and if they were not met, sanction to open to passengers would usually be withheld. The regulations were amended from time to time, this version being current in the early 1900s.

Catchpoints to be provided at junctions of passenger with goods lines or sidings, and interlocked with signals.

Junctions at stations to be formed so as to avoid standing passenger trains on them.

All junctions to be formed for double lines.

At termini, double track lines shall not end single.

Platforms not less than 6 feet wide at small stations, and 12 feet wide at large; ends to be ramped.

Pillars etc to be not less than 6 feet from the edge of platforms.

Height of platform above rail should be 3 feet; in no case to be less than 2ft 6in.

Space between platform and carriage footboards to be as small as possible.

Footbridges or subways at all important stations.

Viaducts near stations to have parapets to prevent passengers alighting and then falling off viaduct.

Staircases or ramps to platforms to be nowhere narrower than at the top.

No steps to have a tread of less than 11in, or a rise of less than 7in.

Landing required where height of steps over 10 feet.

Ramps not to exceed 1 in 8.

No station to be on a grade of less than 1 in 260 if possible; catch points on steeper grades.

Turntables for longest engine at termini, except branches less than 15 miles long, with stations less than 3 miles apart if the company undertake to stop all trains at all stations.

Cast iron must not be used for underbridges except in compression. Breaking weight to be not less than 3x the dead weight plus 6x the live load.

Viaducts as far as possible to be masonry. In all cases there must be a parapet 4ft 6in above rail level. On important viaducts there must be a timber guard close to and outside the outer rails.

Upper surfaces of wood viaducts or bridges to be protected from fire.

Rail joints to be fished.

Chairs on main lines to weigh not less than 40lb; and on minor lines not less than 30lb.

Chairs to be fastened to sleepers by iron spikes or bolts.

Where there are no chairs, fastening to sleeper at joints to be by fang or through bolts, and such rails to be tied to gauge by steel or iron tie rods on curves of 15 chains radius or less.

Check rail to be fixed on all passenger lines where curve is of 10 chains radius or less.

Diamond crossings not to be flatter than a 1 in 8 angle.

No structure other than a platform to be closer to the side of a carriage than 2ft 4in.

Interval between adjacent lines to be not less than 6 feet for two lines or lines and sidings and not less than 9ft 6in between additional running lines and main lines.

Quarter, half and mile posts and gradient posts to be provided.

Tunnels and long viaducts to have refuges for platelayers.

Underbridges without parapets to have handrails.

Viaducts of steel, iron or timber to be easy to inspect.

Opposite page: An angry sky that presaged a violent thunderstorm heightens the dramatic appeal of one of Ireland's most prestigious railway buildings, the Amiens Street headquarters of the erstwhile Great Northern Railway (Ireland). When work began here in 1844, Amiens Street was to be the terminus of the Dublin & Drogheda Railway, but even at this early stage, when it was little more than a local line, and the Irish 'Railway Age' was in its infancy, the promoters must have had some inkling that their railway was destined for greatness. Not only did they employ Ireland's leading architect, William Deane Butler, but the foundation stone was laid by Earl de Grey, the Lord Lieutenant of Ireland on 24th May 1844, the station being completed two years later.

Over the next forty years, the Dublin & Drogheda expanded and merged with other companies, to become part of Ireland's second largest railway company, the Great Northern. Its busy Dublin-Belfast main line and routes that served a great swathe of the north west of Ireland including Armagh, Bundoran, Cavan, Enniskillen, Londonderry, Omagh and Warrenpoint, gave it a financial strength denied to most other Irish railways. It survived as an independent company until 1953, and under the control of the Great Northern Railway Board, jointly financed by the two Irish governments until 1958, when the GNRB was dissolved and its assets were divided between the two nationalised undertakings on either side of the border, the UTA and CIE.

William Deane Butler, who designed this classical Italianate building with its imposing campanile tower was widely regarded as Ireland's leading architect of the period. He trained under the celebrated Henry Aaron Baker at the Dublin Society Schools, and was an engineer as well as an architect. Butler was a founder member of the Royal Institute of Architects in Ireland and whilst Amiens Street station is widely regarded as his finest work, other notable buildings of his include Kilkenny Cathedral and the Sligo Asylum. In 1966, some years after the demise of the GNR(I), Amiens Street station in common with other major stations in the Irish Republic was renamed after one of the leaders of the 1916 Easter Rebellion, becoming Dublin Connolly. The old name is still regularly heard. Amiens Street is actually named in memory of Viscount Amiens, 1st Earl of Aldborough, who resided in this part of Dublin long ago.

GLOSSARY

Abutment	Brick or stone construction taking the vertical and lateral thrust of an arch or beam bridge.
Acanthus Leaf	Thick leafy decoration used in decoration, especially on Corinthian Capitals.
Ashlar	Large smoothly finished and finely jointed squared blocks of stone (also dressed).
Balustrade	An openwork parapet held up by ballusters, usually stone, but can be decorative iron.
Bargeboard	A board attached to the edge of a roof. May be decorated.
Barley twist lamp	A lamp standard with a twisted pattern said to resemble a barley stick sweet.
Batter	A wall that is thicker at the base than the top, the outer face sloping backwards.
Bedstone	Large stone or concrete block on which a bridge girder rests.
Bowstring bridge	A bridge where the girder forms an arc or bow.
Bracket signal	Signal with a horizontal bracket carrying one or more posts offset from the main post.
Bridge rail	Sometimes called top hat rail; it is arch shaped. See page 51 for an illustration of this type of rail.
Bullhead rail	Developed from double headed rail. Supported in chairs, standard UK rail 1840s-1940s.
Campanile	A bell tower commonly found on Italianate structures. In railway usage, it would not ordinarily contain bells, but will often have the row of round headed openings just below the roof line for appearance. See Dublin Amiens Street, page 95.
Cantilever bridge	A bridge consisting of self supporting arms projecting towards one another.
Capital	The top of a column, which can be Greek or Roman Doric, Corinthian, Ionic or Tuscan.
Centering	The wood framework supporting an arch during construction.
Chair	A cast iron base, with shaped jaws, placed on a sleeper to support bullhead rail. Many varieties exist. See pages 50-58 for details of different types. Also known as a rail chair.
Coping stones	Stones on top of a wall or bridge parapet, decorative and to stop ingress of water.
Corbel	A projection from a wall, which can be decorative or used to support a beam.
Corinthian capital	A decorative top to a fluted column, usually decorated with Acanthus leaves.
Cornice	A projecting moulding at the top of a wall or arch.
Cottage orne	Architectural style resurrected c1900; rustic, half timbering, ornate bargeboards.
Crenellated	Resembling the high and low portions of a battlement on a castle.
Cross girder	A girder running at right angles and connecting the main girders.
Dentils	A row of small regularly shaped projecting blocks beneath a cornice.
Domestic revival style	Architectural style popular from 1880s to 1920s, step pitch roofs, overhanging eaves.
Doric capital	A decorative top to a fluted column, usually plain or ringed (Greek or Roman).
Dressed	Large smoothly finished and finely jointed squared blocks of stone (also Ashlar).
Elliptical arch	An arch in the form of an ellipse, or curve that changes radius from gentle to sharp.
Extrados	The upper surface of an arch.
Finial	An ornamental spike or ball on top of a signal post or roof.
Fishbelly	Early rail with straight top, but with the bottom bowing down between rail joints.
Fishplate	A metal plate with four holes used to join lengths of rail together.
Flange	The top and bottom horizontal plates of a girder.
Flatbottom/FB rail	Rail with a flat foot that can rest directly on sleeper or on a bedplate, (Vignoles rail).
Gable roof	A roof where one or more ends is in the form of a vertical triangle.
Hipped roof	A roof with sloping ends rather than vertical gables.
Hogbacked bridge	Like a bowstring, but the curved member is separated by short verticals from straight beam.
Intrados	The lower surface of an arch.
Ionic capital	A decorative top to a fluted column, usually decorated with spirals.

Italianate style	Architectural style with round headed windows, square towers, shallow hipped roofs.
Jack arch	The small brick arches between the girders of a bridge.
Jacobean style	Revival of James II architectural style, curly gables, tall chimneys.
Keystone	The wedge shaped topmost stone in an arch.
Lancet window	Tall narrow window with a pointed arch top.
Lattice girder	A girder consisting of top and bottom horizontal flanges connected by 'X' pattern strips.
Masonry	Work built by a stone mason out of stone, also used for brick.
Mullion	A narrow stone pillar dividing a window.
Overline bridge	A bridge carrying a road or footpath over a railway.
Pandrol clip	Curved spring clip used in baseplate to hold a flatbottom rail in place.
Pantile	A decorative shaped roof tile, often associated with the Italianate style of building, but found with other architectural styles as well.
Parapet	The wall at the side of a bridge to stop pedestrians falling off.
Pier	An intermediate upright upon which the arches or beams of a multi span bridge rest.
Plate girder	A girder composed of a solid vertical plate and top and bottom horizontal flanges.
Porte cochere	A porch, usually glazed at the front of a building under which vehicles unload.
Quatrefoil	Four lobed cut out decoration. See Newtown station, page 38.
Quoins	Decorative stones, alternately long and short at the edge of a building.
Rough hewn	Also rock faced stone; stone as cut at quarry and not given smooth dressing.
Running-in board	The large nameboard at the end of the platform seen by passengers as their train arrives.
Skewback	A shaped stone on which the voussoirs of an arch rest; also see Forth bridge section, page 89.
Skew bridge	A bridge which crosses a road, river or railway at an angle (See page 86).
Span	The distance between the piers or abutments of a bridge.
Spandrel	A bracket projecting from a wall and supporting a projecting canopy., often decorative.
Spandrel wall	The infill between the arch, the abutment and the bottom of the parapet on a bridge.
Stanchion	An upright iron or steel support, often for railings.
String course	A decorative horizontal band of brick or stone along a wall (see Buckby Wharf bridge, pages 82 and 83).
Target	A red board, usually round, but sometimes diamond shaped, attached to a white painted level crossing gate to enhance visibility, also known as gate target.
Trefoil	Three lobed cut out decoration, resembles a three leaf clover. See Newtown station.
Truss	Roof support of timber, iron or steel; also used for lattice or Warren girders.
Tudor style	Revival of Henry VIII architecture style, straight stone gables, tall decorated chimneys.
Tuscan capital	A top to a plain column, with little decoration.
Underline bridge	Bridge beneath the tracks carrying a railway over something.
Valance	The decorative vertical edging timber on a canopy.
Voussoir	Tapered stone blocks that form the arch of a bridge, see Delamere Forest bridge pages 84 and 85.
Warren truss	Girders made from diagonal or triangular sections, invented by James Warren in 1848.
Weatherboarding	Horizontal wood cladding with boards overlapped from above to protect from rain.
Wing walls	Walls that project out at an angle (or curved) from bridge abutment to act as retainers.